The Internet for Windows 95
Made Simple

Made Simple *Computer Books*

● easy to follow   ● jargon free   ● practical   ● task based   ● easy steps

Thousands of people have already discovered that the **MADE SIMPLE** series gives them what they want *fast!* These are the books for you if you want to **learn quickly what's essential** and **how** to do things with a particular piece of software. Many delighted readers have written, telephoned and e-mailed us about the **Made Simple Series** of Computer books. Comments have included:

● "Clear, concise and well laid out"
● "Ideal for the first time user."
● "Clear, accurate, well presented, jargon free, well targeted."
● "Easy to follow to perform a task."
● "I haven't found any other books worth recommending until these."

This **best selling** series is in your **local bookshop now**, or in case of difficulty, contact:

Heinemann Publishers, Oxford, P.O.Box 381,Oxford OX2 8EJ.
Tel 01865 314300. Fax 01865 314091. Credit card sales 01865 314627.

Series titles:

Excel for Windows	Stephen Morris	0 7506 2070 6
Lotus 1-2-3 (DOS)	Ian Robertson	0 7506 2066 8
MS-DOS	Ian Sinclair	0 7506 2069 2
MS-Works for Windows	P. K. McBride	0 7506 2065 X
Windows 3.1	P. K. McBride	0 7506 2072 2
Word for Windows	Keith Brindley	0 7506 2071 4
WordPerfect (DOS)	Stephen Copestake	0 7506 2068 4
Access for Windows	Moira Stephen	0 7506 2309 8
The Internet	P.K.McBride	0 7506 2311 X
Quicken for Windows	Stephen Copestake	0 7506 2308 X
WordPerfect for Windows	Keith Brindley	0 7506 2310 1
Lotus 123 (5.0) for Windows	Stephen Morris	0 7506 2307 1
Multimedia	Simon Collin	0 7506 2314 4
Pageplus for Windows	Ian Sinclair	0 7506 2312 8
Powerpoint	Moira Stephen	0 7506 2420 5
Hard Drives	Ian Robertson	0 7506 2313 6
Windows 95	P.K. McBride	0 7506 2306 3
WordPro	Moira Stephen	0 7506 2626 7
Office 95	P.K. McBride	0 7506 2625 9
The Internet for Windows 95	P.K.McBride	0 7506 2835 9
Word for Windows 95	Keith Brindley	0 7506 2815 4
Excel for Windows 95	Stephen Morris	0 7506 2816 2
Internet Resources	P.K.McBride	0 7506 2836 7
Powerpoint for Windows 95	Moira Stephen	0 7506 2817 0
Microsoft Networking	P.K.McBride	0 7506 2837 5
Designing Internet Home Pages	Lilian Hobbs	0 7506 2941 X
Access for Windows 95	Moira Stephen	0 7506 2818 9

The Internet for Windows 95 Made Simple

P.K.McBride

MADE SIMPLE
BOOKS

Made Simple
An imprint of Butterworth-Heinemann
Linacre House, Jordan Hill, Oxford OX2 8DP
A division of Reed Educational and Professional Publishing Ltd

ℝ   A member of the Reed Elsevier plc group

OXFORD   BOSTON   JOHANNESBURG
MELBOURNE   NEW DELHI   SINGAPORE

First published 1996
© P.K.McBride 1996

TRADEMARKS/REGISTERED TRADEMARKS
Computer hardware and software brand names mentioned in this book are protected
by their respective trademarks and are acknowledged.

British Library Cataloguing in Publication Data
A catalogue record for this book is available from the British Library

ISBN 0 7506 2835 9

Typeset by P.K.McBride, Southampton

Archtype, Bash Casual, Cotswold and Gravity fonts from Advanced Graphics Ltd
Icons designed by Sarah Ward © 1994

Printed and bound in Great Britain by Scotprint, Musselburgh, Scotland

Contents

The Internet is vast, varied and changing fast. This book concentrates on the most accessible parts, and those aspects that will be of interest to most people – electronic mail, newsgroups, downloading files and browsing the World Wide Web.

The best way to get to grips with the Internet is to explore it. But exploration can take you into dead ends or round in circles. This book aims to provide you with a map, and some of the basic tools, so that you don't get (too) lost.

The first four sections cover the preparations to be made while still at the base camp. They provide a crash course in the native language of the Internet, its key concepts and jargon, and look at the equipment that you will need for your expedition.

The next three sections start you off down alternative routes into the Internet, through Compuserve, the IBM PC User Group and Total Connectivity Providers, each of which has its own distinctive characteristics.

The final sections explore the World Wide Web and other sources of files and information on the Internet.

Windows 95

Windows 95 has its own built in tools for accessing the Internet. These tools have been used in preparing this book – but note that almost everything done via Windows 95 can be done equally well (and sometimes more easily) via Windows 3.1.

MSN

The Microsoft Network was launched alongside Windows 95, but at the time of writing was still in beta-test mode. It clearly has potential, but until it has established a network of fast local dialup points, and can offer full access to the Internet, it cannot compete with established services.

1 Internet FAQs

What is it?

The Internet is not a single network, but a collection of thousands of computer networks, throughout the world. These vary greatly in size and in the number of computers that are connected to them. These linked networks are of two types:

- **LAN** (Local Area Network), covering an office or perhaps a campus;

- **WAN** (Wide Area Network), joining distant sites. A WAN may extend over the whole country, or even over many countries.

All LANs and most WANs are owned by individual organisations. Some WANs act as **Service Providers**. Members of the public and/or businesses can join these networks – usually in return for a modest charge.

The computers likewise vary from giant supercomputers down to desktop computers – PC's, Macintoshes, Amigas, Archimedes or whatever. They are owned and run by thousands of separate universities, government agencies, businesses and individuals.

There is no central authority or governing body, though there is an Internet Society, established a couple of years ago to co-ordinate and standardise rules of operation. The Internet relies on co-operation, driven by goodwill and enlightened self-interest. And it works!

Jargon

FAQ (Frequently Asked Questions) At every place on the Internet where you can ask for help, someone keeps a FAQ list. This is a set of common questions, and their answers. It is good form to check the FAQ first, before asking your own question.

Network A collection of computers, linked by cable or radio. On a LAN these can share the printers, modems and other resources that are attached to the network. On any network – including the Interent – users can communicate easily with each other, and share data held in each others' files.

Service Provider – an organisation offering access to some or all of the services available over the Internet.

Who's on-line?

Take note

The information printed here may be out of date. Anything you read anywhere about the Internet may be out of date. It changes so rapidly, and there are so many people involved in creating new services and in devising new uses for it, that by the time anything gets printed, it may well have been overtaken by events.

If you want to now what's happening NOW, join the Internet and watch the changes from the inside.

Some would say "Everybody who's anybody", but that's not true – yet! So who is on-line on the Internet?

- **Academics**: Students and staff at universities, colleges – and some schools – throughout the world. These form the largest and most active group of users. Apart from the fact that they use the Internet for their studies, they will also not normally have to pay the phone bills.

- **Business users**: many multi-national companies have discovered that the Internet provides the most efficient and cheapest way of communicating with colleagues around the world. An increasing number of companies are also realising that it is a viable way to sell goods and services.

- **Government organisations**: some use the Internet for their own communications; some to make information available to the public. The White House is on line, though 10 Downing Street is not – at the time of writing.

- **Individuals**: anyone with a computer, modem and phone line can join the Internet through one of the public Service Providers. Millions have already linked up. In the UK at the present, around 10,000 new subscribers are coming on-line each month, and the rate of growth is increasing.

What's in it for me?

If you have access to the Internet, you have access to:

- **5 million host computers**, all of which are possible sources of information that could be useful to you in your work, your travelling, your academic research or your hobbies.

- **35+ million people**, any of whom could be future friends, customers, fellow enthusiasts, problem-solvers. There may well even be a few old friends out there already.

- **gigabytes of files** containing programs – including the software that you need for working on the Internet – books, news articles, pictures – still and video – sounds and much else.

- **a whole raft of services**, such as financial advice, stock market information, airline times and reservations, weather reports, small-ads and electronic shopping malls.

Where do I start?

Here, of course. Read on to get an idea of what's going on out there, then learn how to set up your hardware. After that, you should aim to get on-line with one or other of the service providers. There are examples of connecting to and using Compuserve, WinNET, the Microsoft Network and other services, in sections 5, 6 and 7, and a list of UK service providers on page 138.

a list of UK service providers on page 138.

Jargon

Host computer – one that allows Internet users access to (some of) its files.

Gigabyte – a thousand megabytes or 1,000,000,000 bytes. Taking each byte as a letter, this is the equivalent of around 2,000 thick paperback books.

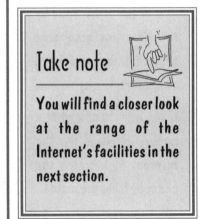

Take note

You will find a closer look at the range of the Internet's facilities in the next section.

How did it start?

Usenet – still a significant name on the Internet. The Usenet news groups make up the greater part of all the Internet's meeting places.

NSFnet – the (US) National Science Foundation's internetwork. The high-speed cables between its sites formed the backbone of the Internet in North America.

Appropriate Use rules – most of us are grateful for these, as they prevent us from being bombarded with advertising over the mailing lists.

The history of the Internet is interesting, but there is no room here to go into any details, and you want to use the Internet, not write essays on its history. However, there are a few things you should know, as they help to explain aspects of the present.

The Internet story starts with ARPAnet, a long-distance computer network devised by the US Government's Advanced Research Projects Agency. From an initial 4 computers in 1969, this grew over the next 10 years to connect 200 computers in military and research establishments throughout the US, with a few overseas links. It proved, beyond doubt, the practicality and the value of internetworking. By the mid 80's several academic internetworks, including **Usenet**, BITnet, CSnet and **NSFnet** had been set up. These combined with the research part of ARPAnet, to form the Internet.

The crucial point is that the core of the Internet was – and still is – government-funded research or academic organisations. It was not set up as a commercial proposition, and commercial activities on the Internet are a recent innovation. There are still **Appropriate Use** rules that restrict the use of the Internet for profit.

The second historical fact is that the Internet originally linked mainframe computers, most of which ran the Unix operating system. PCs, Macintoshes and other personal computers only came onto the Internet later. As a result, the Internet has a distinct Unix flavour about it. You can do everything from a PC – and there are some lovely Windows tools coming on stream – but sometimes you might have to use Unix commands.

How big?!

Because of the number of different organisations involved, no one knows for sure how big the Internet really is. Five years ago there were around 100,000 host computers connected to the Internet. It reached 500,000 by mid 1991 and has been doubling every year since. At the time of writing (late 1995) the total is close to 4 million – and these are just the *host* computers, the ones that provide services to the Internet.

If you look at the number of people who link into the Internet, either from their desktop machines or from a terminal in a large organisation, the best guess is that there are over 35 million of us, with more joining every day. If the number of users continues to grow at its current rate, everyone in the World will be on the Internet in about 10 years. I don't quite think so...

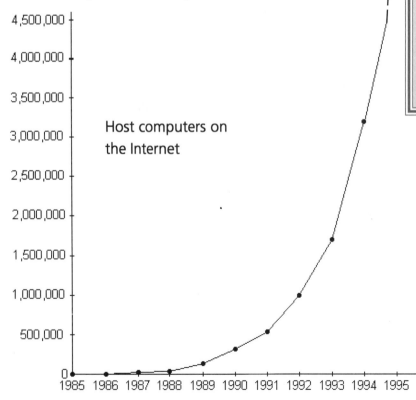

Host computers on
the Internet

Tip

If you feel overwhelmed by the sheer scale of things, remember that you don't need to know the UK road map to find your way from London to Leeds. If you keep your eyes open, you will see signposts to point the route, and if you do get lost, call out for help. There are lots of more experienced users willing to act as guides.

The Internet is growing so rapidly, this graph could be off the top of the page by the time you read it!

In the UK, over 250,000 people are already on-line from their home computers, plus many more through companies, universities and other organisations.

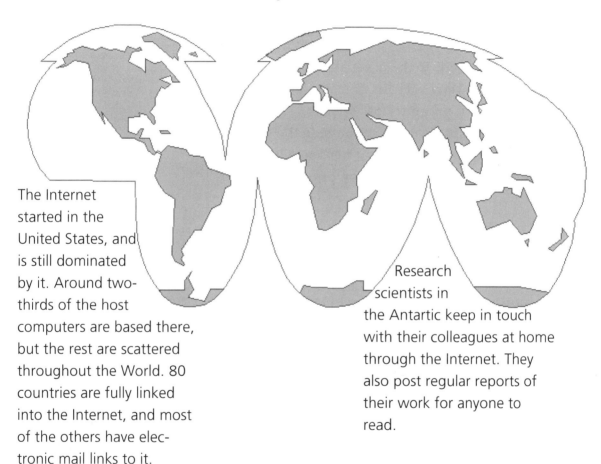

The Internet started in the United States, and is still dominated by it. Around two-thirds of the host computers are based there, but the rest are scattered throughout the World. 80 countries are fully linked into the Internet, and most of the others have electronic mail links to it.

Research scientists in the Antartic keep in touch with their colleagues at home through the Internet. They also post regular reports of their work for anyone to read.

How do I find people?

With something as large as the Internet, it is clear that you need a well-organised naming system to find your way round. Every host computer and network has its own unique name – it also has a number, but on the rare occasions that you need it, someone will tell you what it is. Computers and smaller networks within larger ones may also have their own names, and every user has an address.

Names have several parts to them, separated by dots. The parts are sometimes referred to as **domains**, and they are nested. The last part, or outermost domain, is the zone, which identifies either the country (outside the USA) or the type of organisation. The rest of the name is usually derived directly from the name of the organisation. For example:

> vnet.ibm.com

The *vnet* network within *IBM*, a *com*mercial organisation.

> bhein.rel.co.uk

The *Butterworth-Heine*mann domain, within *Reed El*sevier, a *com*mercial organisation based in the *UK*.

> gn.apc.org

GreenNet, a member of the *A*ssociation for *P*rogressive *C*ommunications *org*anisation.

> sussex.ac.uk

Sussex University (academic) in the *UK*

> oregon.uoregon.edu

The main *Oregon* site in the *U*niversity of *Oregon* (USA).

Zone name examples

com or **co**	commercial
edu or **ac**	educational
net	network provider
org	non-commercial organisation
gov	government depart-ment
uk	United Kingdom
aus	Australia
fr	France
ger	Germany

Take note

As the Internet links up many other networks which have their own addressing systems, some addresses are more complicated than the simple pattern shown here. If you come across an address that you need to use, copy it *very* carefully.

E-mail addresses

Tip

There are some utilities on the Internet that will help you to find people's e-mail addresses, but the simplest way to do it is to phone them and ask them to e-mail to you. Every mail message carries its sender's address.

These follow the host name conventions, but with the user's name at the start, separated by an @ sign. Here, for example, are some of the names that I have had while researching this book. Notice the variations.

macbride@macdesign.win-uk.net

WinNet allocates domains (*macdesign*) to its users, as well as names (*macbride*).

macbride@tcp.co.uk

At *Total Connectivity Providers*, users are simply given names.

100407.2521@compuserv.co.uk

When I joined *CompuServe* it gave its users numbers, rather than names. At the time of writing, it was planning to start using names in the near future.

These names are all from service providers, but the same conventions apply for people in commercial and other organisations. For example, if you wanted to e-mail my editor – perhaps to ask about some other Made Simple books – his address is:

Mike.Cash@bhein.rel.co.uk

URL's

Every file on the Internet has its own URL – Uniform Resource Locator – which tells you what it is called, where to find it and how to get it. We will be using two types in this book – for ftp file transfer (see page 18) and for the World Wide Web (see page 22).

Summary

- ❏ The Internet is a collection of **interlinked networks**, working together co-operatively.

- ❏ You may be able **get into the Internet** either through your business or academic network, but if not, anyone can get a connection through a public **service provider**.

- ❏ You can often find the answers to your problems in the **FAQ** (Frequently Asked Questions) lists maintained for most aspects of the Internet.

- ❏ The Internet gives you access to people, information, files and a vast range of services.

- ❏ **Estimates of the numbers** of networks, computers and people joined by the Internet can never be that accurate, as it is growing faster than anyone can count.

- ❏ Every network, computer and individual on the Internet has a unique **address**.

- ❏ Files are identified by **URLs** (Uniform Resource Locators). These show where the file is, what it is called, and what method to use to find them.

2 Internet services

Electronic mail

These are messages sent to other individuals on the Internet. Think of them more like memos than postal mail. A message can be easily copied to other users; and when you receive an incoming message, you can attach your reply to it, or forward it on to a third party. You can also attach documents and graphics files to messages. (See *Binaries by mail*, page 132.)

The mail will sometimes get through almost instantaneously, but at worst it will be there within a few hours. The delay is because not all networks are constantly on-line. Instead, they will **log on** at regular intervals to deal with the mail and other services.

Key points about e-mail

● Even the simplest connection to the Internet can handle e-mail.

● Every service provider offers **e-mail** access.

● The cheapest and normally most convenient way of handling mail is through an **off-line reader**.

● As with snail mail, to send someone e-mail you need their address. (See *How do I find people?*, page 8)

Log on – connect to a multi-user computer, either directly or over a phone line.

E-mail – electronic mail.

Snail mail – the good old postal service.

Off-line reader – software that sends and collects mail from the service provider, and lets you read it and compose new messages after you have hung up the phone.

Take note

There are many organised **MAIL LISTS** on the Internet, each dealing with its own topic of interest. Subscribers can post messages to a central point, from which they are sent out in a block to all other subscribers. As a means of sharing ideas, they are very similar to Newsgroups – see the next page.

An example of mail seen in WinNET's off-line reader.
This Windows software offers very comprehensive and
easy to use mail-management facilities.

Messages can be stored
in other directories

Call to collect
and send mail

Options for dealing
with incoming mail

This system also gives you
access to newsgroups

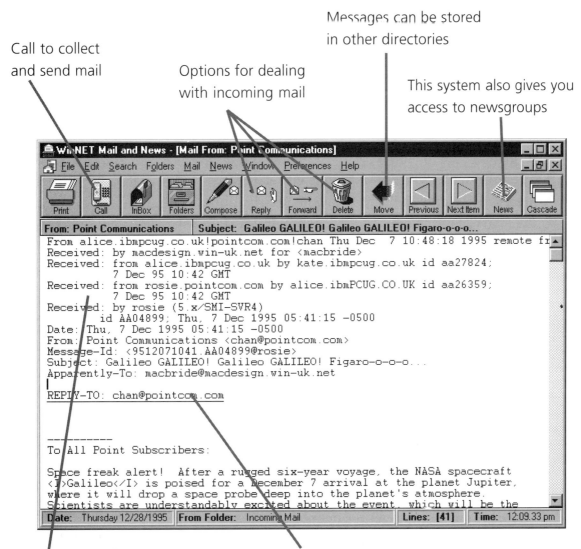

The header details the
origins of the mail

Once someone has contacted you, it is easy to get back to
them as you have their address. This one came from Point
Communications. If you subscribe to their (free) service, you
get regular updates of new developments on the Internet.

News

These have developed from e-mail, and consist of groups of users linked so that an **article** sent to the group is **posted** to all its members. There are thousands of groups, each dedicated to a different interest – professions and obsessions, programming languages and TV programs, software, hobbies, politics.

Key Points about Newsgroups

● Joining a group is easy, free of charge and free of entry restrictions.

● The quality and quantity of the communications vary enormously. Some newsgroups circulate large volumes of interesting and relevant information; others carry few articles – or few of any interest.

● Some newsgroups are moderated, i.e. they have someone who checks all incoming articles before broadcasting them to the members. This reduces the quantity of irrelevant and/or boring post.

● The seedier and steamier side of the Internet is mainly in the newsgroups. If you do not want anyone to access this from your system, there are programs that will filter it out for you.

● Some groups are mainly for discussions, others are more like open help-lines, where people can ask for – and get – solutions to technical problems.

● As newsgroups bring together people who share a common interest, they can be a good place to make new friends.

● If you decide that a newsgroup is not for you, you can leave at any time.

Article – message sent to a newsgroup.

Post – submit an article for broadcasting.

Take note

Most newsgroups are part of USENET – the Users Network – a loose collection of individuals and organisations. Other old networks brought their own groups into the Internet as well. Not all newsgroups can be accessed from all entry points to the Internet.

Usenet

comp   Computing
news   Newsgroups
misc   miscellaneous
rec   Recreational
sci   Scientific
soc   Social and cultural
talk   Debate-oriented

Other

alt   all kinds of topics
biz   business
gnu   Unix systems
bionet academic/scientific
uk   UK-based

... and more...

Newsgroups are organised into a branching structure, with major sections sub-divided by topic. Their names reflect this structure.

For example, *comp.lang.c++* is in the *comp*uter section, which, amongst other topics, covers programming *languages*, including *c++*.

●   Join *news.announce.newusers* as soon as you get a chance. It is specially for those new to the Internet.

(See *Newsgroup subscription*, page 86, *Forums*, page 66.)

Drop-down list of main headings and keywords.

A good system makes it easy to find a newsgroup that interests you. This is one of the tools supplied by WinNET.

There is an **alt** newsgroup for every interest, occupation and obsession

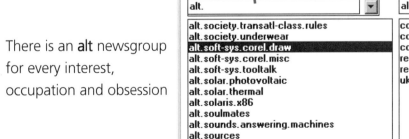

Netiquette

Newsgroups have their own etiquette, and you would do well to observe it if you don't want to be shot down in **flames**. The key is to remember that any article that you post to the newsgroup will be received by all of its members – hundreds, or even thousands of people – and that it will cost each of these phone time to receive it and personal time to read it. As some service providers charge for mail and article storage, it can also cost money.

If a newsgroup has 1,000 members (many have more), a 1kb article takes up 1Mb of net traffic and disk space. Even if members only scan the Subject line, and do not read it, the total time spent will be a couple of man hours.

Key points of netiquette

● When you first join a newsgroup, **lurk** for a while. Read its articles to get a feel of its flavour and level.

● Before you post any questions of your own, read the **FAQs**. These are usually circulated regularly.

● If you post a reply to an article, trim out any unnecessary text, to save everyone's time and **bandwidth**.

● If your reply will only really be interesting to the original author, e-mail it, don't post it.

● Keep your own postings brief and to the point.

Bandwidth – strictly the capacity of the comms lines, but taken to mean on-line time/ mailbox storage.

FAQ – Frequently Asked Questions, and their answers. A great source of information.

Flame – overreaction to a breach of netiquette or tactless remark. Can lead to **flame wars** if the victims believe they are right.

Lurk – read articles, without posting. There's nothing wrong with lurking.

Reply – send an email in reply to an article, rather than posting the reply to the group.

Tip

Join news.announce.newusers for advice for new users, and look out for Emily Postnews' Etiquette for USENET News Postings. It's circulated fairly often.

An example of an article and its posted reply,
from the *comp.unix.questions* newsgroup.

Your newsreader will
show the subject line
in a list of articles. You
can then ignore those
that do not interest
you.

The original article

Smiley! This is a joke.

From: magnus@thakhasis.solace.mh.se (Magnus Nasholm)
Newsgroups: comp.unix.questions
Subject: Re: protecting my e-mail
Date: 9 Dec 1994 19:08:14 +0100
Organization: Solace Computer Club, Sundsvall, Sweden
Lines: 12
Message-ID: <magnus.786995925@thakhasis>
References: <3c79fs$ji0@sparc.occ.uky.edu>
NNTP-Posting-Host: thakhasis.solace.mh.se

REPLY-TO: magnus@thakhasis.solace.mh.se

jackswe@ndlc.occ.uky.edu (Wayne Jackson) writes:

>I know of someone that can read my mail on the internet.
>Is there anyway to keep this from happening.

Don't send them to him... ;-)

No, but in fact it is very hard to keep users with the right
priviledge from reading them (root, for example). If it is a
unprivileged user doing this you should check the permissions
on your mailbox.
However I've got the feeling that anyone can listen to the
network and read mail in that way, at least in their domain.

Tip

**If you are joking, and want to make sure
that your readers know it is a joke, add a
smiley :-) or <grin> or <g>.**

File transfer

There are gigabytes of files are stored out there, just waiting to be **downloaded**. They include the latest updates of applications software, pictures from high art to low pornography, recipes, TV guides, news articles and all sorts of texts. Also there, are the tools you need for using the Internet, along with guides on how to use them.

Service providers have their own stores of files, and to get one of these, you usually just select from a list. Once you are into the Internet, you have access to all the millions of other files on host computers all over the world. These can obtained by **ftp** – file **t**ransfer **p**rotocol.

Key points about ftp

● To do ftp directly, you must have an interactive connection to the Internet. This will let you connect to the host, search its directories and get files. (See *Go ftp*, page 70 and *ftp the easyway*, page 102.)

● If you do not have a direct connection, ftp can also be done by mail. (See *ftp by mail*, page 130.)

● To ftp a file, you must know where it is stored, and what it is called. (See next page.)

● When ftp'ing to a site, you usually login in as **anonymous**, giving your user name as the password.

Downloading – transferring a file from a distant computer onto your machine.

Uploading – sending files from your computer to the on-line host, for others to download .

ftp (File Transfer Protocol) – a nifty piece of software that can copy files between different types of computers. You need to be able to use ftp if you are to get files from anywhere other than the main data banks of your service provider.

Take note

ftp URL's look like this:

ftp://ftp.temple.edu/pub/info/help-net/babel95c.txt

use ftp	address	path to directory	filename

This URL is for *Babel*, a glossary of computer acronyms and abbreviations. New versions appear regularly, but the name is always 'babel' followed by the year number and then 'a', 'b' or 'c'. Get it, read it and baffle your friends.

This screenshot is from an interactive session using WS-ftp.
It uses standard Windows techniques to change directories,
and select files.

The remote system is at Imperial College, London
(Sunsite UK), and I'm connected to one of their
public sub-directories

This pane shows the
directory and files on
my system

Clicking here will
copy the selected
file into my system.

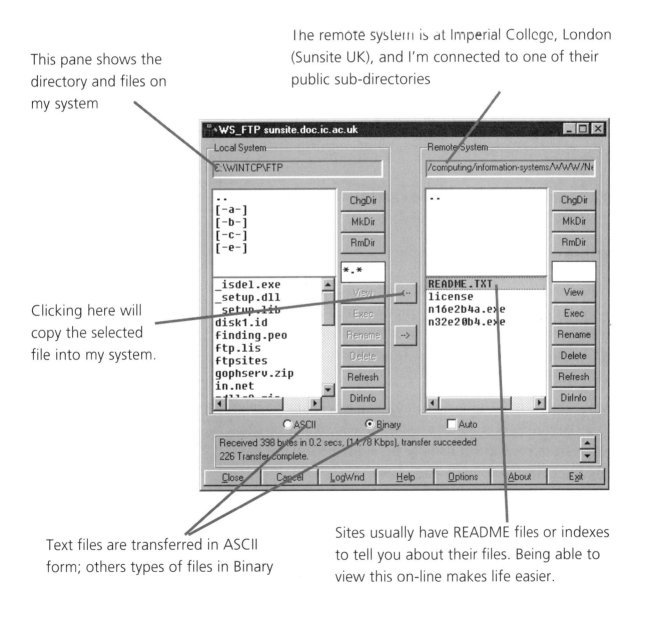

Text files are transferred in ASCII
form; others types of files in Binary

Sites usually have README files or indexes
to tell you about their files. Being able to
view this on-line makes life easier.

Finding files

This isn't as hard as it may at first appear. There are a number of ways to find files.

- **ftp** can also be used to tell you the contents of a directory, so once you have found a site, you can see what is there.

- **Members of newsgroups** will regularly alert other members of the arrival of a new and interesting file.

- **Browsing the World Wide Web**, you will often come across references to files, along with their ftp details.

- There is a program called **Archie** which will search the world's archives for you.

Archie

The search program is actually run on an **archie server** – a remote computer – not on your own PC. To do an archie search, you must **telnet** to a server (tricky), or use WS_archie or similar software to handle the connections for you (much easier).

Archie can also be done by **e-mail**. You can mail a request to an archie server to find a file for you. A list of sites where it is stored will usually be mailed back the next day. (See *Archie by mail*, page 128)

Archie – a file-finding utility. If you know the name of a file, or at least part of its name, then Archie can tell you where you can find a copy that you can collect by ftp.

Archie server – host computer that has the search software and database, and that allows users to perform searches.

Telnet – a method of accessing remote computers, to run Archie, play games or use other programs on the remote system. This can only be done if your service provider has an interactive connection to the Internet.

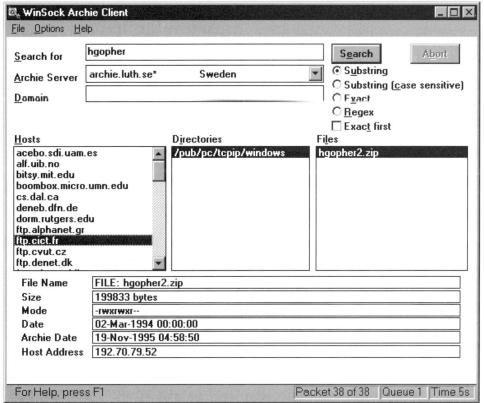

Finding a file
with WS_archie

Part of an archie reply to an e-mailed request to find uuencode, a program for converting binary files so that they can be sent by mail. Where there are several copies, you should get the one closest to you.

```
>> find uuencode.com
# Search type: sub.

Host nic.switch.ch    (130.59.10.40)
Last updated 04:13 25 Oct 1994

    Location: /mirror/msdos/starter
      FILE    -rw-rw-r--    997 bytes  11:07  5 Oct 1994  uuencode.com

Host micros.hensa.ac.uk    (148.88.8.84)
Last updated 03:30 29 Oct 1994

    Location: /mirrors/simtel/msdos/starter
      FILE    -r--r--r--    997 bytes  09:07  5 Oct 1994  uuencode.com

Host src.doc.ic.ac.uk    (146.169.43.1)
Last updated 08:30 31 Oct 1994

    Location: /computing/systems/ibmpc/simtel/starter
      FILE    -r--r--r--    964 bytes  09:07  5 Oct 1994  uuencode.com.Z
```

The World Wide Web

The World Wide Web is a collection of pages, stored on computers throughout the world, and joined by **hypertext** links. It is the newest and the fastest-growing part of the Internet. Its rapid leap into popularity stems largely from the ease with which Web-browsing software, such as Mosaic and Netscape, can be used.

- The pages cover virtually every service and information source that is on the Internet.

- With a **Web browser** and some extra graphics/sound software, you can view pictures in exhibitions and live photographs from cameras attached to the Internet, watch clips from videos, or listen to music.

- Some pages have files linked to them, and these can be downloaded directly; others may tell you where to find interesting or useful files.

- To browse the Web, your service provider must give you an interactive (**SLIP** or **PPP**) connection.

Hypertext – documents linked so that clicking on a button, icon or keyword takes you into the related document – wherever it may be. Web pages are written in **HTML** (HyperText Markup Language) that handles links in a standardised way.

Web browser – program that lets you leap between hypertext links to read text, view graphics and videos, and hear sounds.

Mosaic – one of the first, and until recently, the best Web browser. Now challenged by **Netscape.**

SLIP – Serial Line Interface Protocol

PPP – Point-to-Point Protocol.

It makes no difference whether you use a SLIP or a PPP connection. Both support the same software.

Take note

World Wide Web URL's look like this:

http://www.findme.com/findme/index.html

use the Web to get this

Web page (combined address, path and filename)

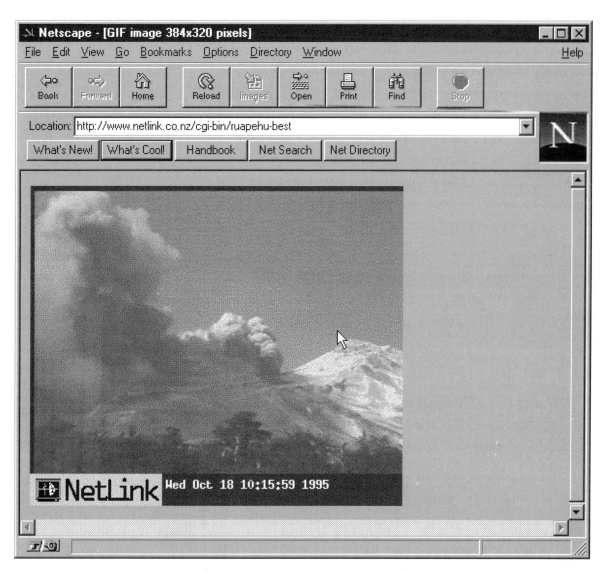

There are many interesting devices attached to the Web, including over 100 cameras. Some of these are 'spy cameras' that peek into an office or laboratory.

Some are windows onto the world. This picture comes from a camera close by Mt Ruapehu, an active volcano in New Zealand. A new picture is taken every few minutes.

Other devices include robot arms, a geiger counter and a hot-tub's thermometer. The practical value is often nil, but they are a marvellous indication of what can be done over the Net.

Gopher

Gopher is a **menu-driven** program that links many of the Internet's databanks into a unified information service. It was developed at the University of Minnesota, home of the Golden Gophers sports team and its name is relection of this and a pun on *go-for*. For a couple of years, until the development of the World Wide Web, it was the way to travel the Internet, and some people still prefer it to Web-browsing. The original gopher has been augmented by *gopher plus*, with some added facilities, and new Windows software for gophering handles most of the technicalities for you.

- The menus follow a standard pattern, with items leading either to the next level of menus or to items. You may sometimes go through many levels of menus to get to a specific article.

- Items may be text, graphic or sound files.

- There is a vast amount of information in **gopherspace**, but it's well organised, so that you can generally find what you want with little trouble.

- There are subject and regional catalogues as well as reference sources and *Gopher Jewels* – a collection of some of the most interesting gopher sources.

- If you don't fancy hunting through menus, there is a program called *Veronica*, which can track topics down for you.

- A good Windows gopher will handle the URL's for you – which is just as well, as they are not simple to manage for yourself!

Gopherspace – sometimes used to describe the thousands of computers and their files that are linked through the gopher menus.

Menu-driven – where you select from a list, often working down through several lists until you have focussed on the thing you want.

> ## Take note
>
> You don't need special software to access the information in the gopher system. It can all can be reached through the World Wide Web, using a standard Web browser.

The screen from HGOPHER, a Windows gopher program. Selections are made by clicking on the name of an entry.

When you reach a gopher menu that you want to come back to regularly, you can record it as a Bookmark. Next time you want to go there, you can leap straight to it.

Back to the last menu

Down to a lower level menu

Search routine

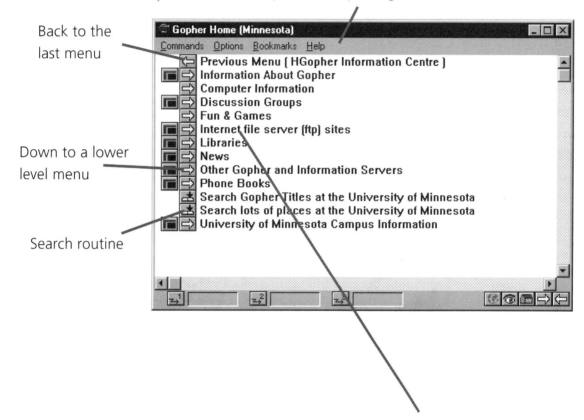

FTP servers, and other Internet facilities can also be accessed easily through the gopher menus.

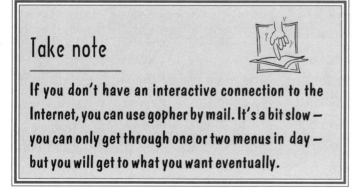

Take note

If you don't have an interactive connection to the Internet, you can use gopher by mail. It's a bit slow – you can only get through one or two menus in day – but you will get to what you want eventually.

MSN (Microsoft Network)

At the time of writing MSN – the Microsoft Network – was still in its trial stage and had set a limit of 500,000 members. This limit was probably not necessary, as – at present – MSN does not yet offer much that you cannot get better, easier and cheaper elsewhere. But don't write them off. Microsoft has the skills, the marketing muscle and the money to become a major player in this field.

The big plus about MSN is its simplicity of use. Configuration is very simple, and largely done for you. Once you get on-line and past the top-level pages, moving around the Network and selecting activities is very similar to working within your own system.

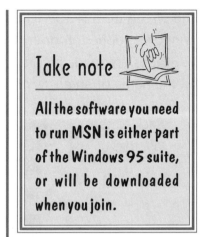

Take note

All the software you need to run MSN is either part of the Windows 95 suite, or will be downloaded when you join.

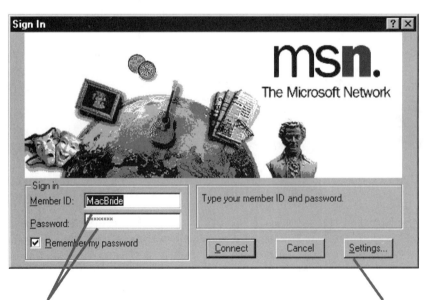

You can store your ID and password, so that you can sign in at the panel simply by clicking Connect. (It's a good idea to write down your password somewhere safe, in case you ever need it – you can't read it off the screen!)

The main use of the Settings button is to change the dial-in number to one close to you. There were 50 local access points in the UK at the time of writing.

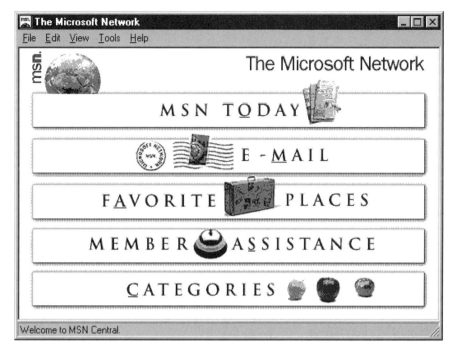

MSN goes in for graphical screens – pretty, but slow to download. Typical time from sign-in to starting work is up to 3 minutes – mainly waiting for pictures!

E-mail is run through Microsoft Exchange – get it running before you go on-line.

The folder-based approach is used in the working areas below the top level menus. If you can use Explorer, you should be able to navigate your way round MSN without any trouble.

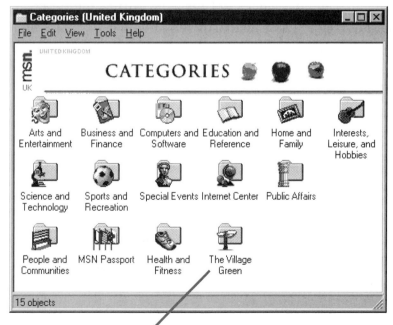

The range of interests catered for by MSN is increasing steadily. Three months from launch, we have all these categories, most of which lead to quite extensive areas.

The Village Green is a central point for UK users. It even has a pub and a tea-shop!

Other services

Interactive services

Some of these are available to any user over the World Wide Web, others can only be accessed through a communications services like CompuServe. With a credit card to hand, you can book travel and theatre tickets, make hotel reservations, order flowers, chocolates, books, software and lots else besides.

Games

There are also interactive games which many people can play at once, pitting their wits against distant, unseen, opponents. The original, **MUD**, has now been joined by many others. At the time of writing, DOOM, a highly graphical, multi-level 3-D shoot-'em-up, is the main focus for most on-line games enthusiasts; with a multi-player aerial combat game also providing much excitement and frustration.

Chat lines

These are the on-line equivalent of CB radio, with typing replacing talking. The 'chat' varies from academic discussions to gossip between friends.

There is much overlapping between categories. In CompuServe, for example, there are many Forums for different interests. As a member of a forum you can download files from its library, read messages or join an on-line conference.

MUD – Multi-User Dungeons and Dragons. A role-playing game where on-line players cooperate or compete to win.

Tip

There have been several cases of people running scams and hacking into credit card databases over the Internet. Security is improving, but take care over who you give your credit card details to.

This illustration came from Microsoft's Internet Explorer, one of the Web browsers used in researching this book.

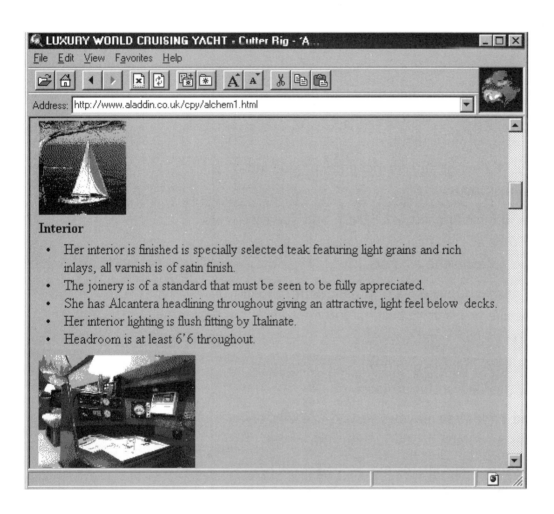

Yes, you can even shop for a yacht on-line. This is from Carl Phillips on-line Yacht Brokerage, a service run from Aladdin's Sonet. There are full-colour interior and exterior shots, with full descriptions of their stock. By the way, this little number is yours for a mere $795,000!

Summary

- ☐ **E-mail** is cheaper and faster than the post.

- ☐ E-mail can be sent to individuals, or to a group, organised into a **mail list**.

- ☐ **Off-line readers** are the most convenient way to deal with mail.

- ☐ **Newsgroups** provide meeting points for people who share a common profession, interest or obsession. There are thousands of them!

- ☐ The names of newsgroups are generally a good indication of their focus.

- ☐ Most newsgroups are part of **USENET**, and open to anyone. Some are run from other networks, and are not always accessible to all users.

- ☐ Lurk in a newsgroup and learn its **netiquette** (and its jargon) before you start to post, or you may get caught up in a flame war.

- ☐ You can transfer files to and from host computers using **ftp**, the file transfer protocol.

- ☐ The **World Wide Web** provides easy-to-use links between files on computers throughout the World.

- ☐ **Web browsers** are programs that let you travel read and view files on the World Wide Web. Mosaic and Netscape are the two most commonly used.

- ☐ **Gopher** is an earlier method of linking and locating files on the Internet. It is particularly useful for academic research.

- ☐ Games, chat lines and a range of interactive services are also available over the Internet.

3 Basic communications

Hardware

To get on-line, you need three items of hardware – a computer, a modem and a phone connection.

The computer

Almost any type of machine is suitable. People are using everything from massive mainframes down to ancient Commodore 64s. For the individual user, life is probably simplest from a PC or Apple Macintosh, as there is the greatest choice of commercial and free software tools for these. Business users and students and staff in schools and colleges, will probably find themselves working with networked PCs or terminals of a large computer. These should not present any problems. Suitable communications software is available for all major networks and large computer systems.

If you only intend to use the Internet for e-mail and transferring files, a text-based terminal or a slow old computer will do the job – it will still work fast enough to keep up with the flow of data over the phone line. If you want to explore the World Wide Web, or play interactive graphics games, then you must have a reasonably fast machines that can handle high-resolution graphics.

The research for this book was done on a 486 PC, using Windows 95. Windows make Internet working easier, just as it makes most jobs easier. The connectivity tools built into Windows 95 can make some things even simpler.

Phone connection

❑ All that is essential here is that you have a socket within reach of your desktop. If you haven't, any good DIY store will supply you with an extension kit and wall-mounted socket.

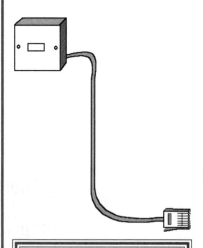

Take note

Using Windows 95 to connect to the Microsoft Network is very simple – but connecting to any other service can be tricky. See page 96.

Modem – MOdulator/
DEModulator. A device
that converts digital
signals from a
computer into analogue
ones for transmission
over the phone lines
(and *vice versa*).

CCITT – the consultative
committee that sets
standards for interna-
tional telegraphy and
telecommunications.

The modem

The type of modem dictates the speed with which you can transfer data to and from the Internet. The faster it is, the lower your phone bills will be, and its speed depends on two things – baud rate and data compression.

Baud rate

This is the number of *bits* per second (bps) that can be pushed down the line.The baud rates supported by a modem are defined by the CCITT standards (the V numbers). If you don't know what rates yours will handle, but do know its V number, look up the rates in this table.

Standard	Baud rates
V.21	300
V.22	1200
V.22bis	2400
V.23	1200/75
V.32	4800, 9600
V.32bis	4800, 7200, 9600, 12000, 14400
V.fast	as V32 bis plus 28,800

Take note

No matter how fast your modem, you may still find that data trickles in from busy sites at busy times of day. When it's really bad, the rate can drop below 500 bytes per second.

There are 8 bits to a byte, but all transmissions have extra addressing and error-checking information attached to them, so divide by 10 to get an idea of the *bytes* per second speed, or by 10,000 to get the Kilobyte rate.

300 Baud = 30 bytes per second = 1Kb every 33 seconds

9600 Baud = 1Kb per second, approx.

28,800 Baud = 3Kb per second = 1Mb every 6 minutes

Data compression

The same kind of data compression techniques that allow Stacker to cram twice as much data on your hard disk, allow modems to push data through faster. On modems, they are usually merged with error correction techniques. There are two standards – MNP and V.42bis, offering compression from 2:1 up to 4:1. Both are widely used, and many current modems support both standards.

Data compression does not always give faster through-put. It basically works by replacing repeated bytes (or patterns of bytes) by one copy of the byte plus a count of the repetitions. It therefore works best with text files, where blocks of spaces and repeated patterns are common. It does not work well with executable files, where repetition is rare, and if the file is already compressed then further 'compression' can actually make it bigger! Most picture formats have some sort of compression built into them, and many of the text files available for downloading over the Internet are ZIPped.

If you want to test the effects of compression, get a copy of PKZIP (see page 140), and try ZIPping files of different types. You should find that compression ranges from 90% or more, down to 5% - you may even find that some small files produce larger 'compressed' files!

Take note

A 1Mb file will take over an hour to download with a 2400 baud modem, or under 5 minutes with a 28,800 modem using V.42 bis data compression. How much a minute do your phone calls cost?

MNP – Microcom Network Protocol. Microcom is one of the leading data comms companies.

ZIP – extension given to files that have been compressed by the PKZIP utility. You need PKUNZIP, or WINZIP to restore these to their proper state.

Port – connection between the computer and the outside world.

Serial port – transmits data one bit after another down a single line. Communications are almost always done via a serial port.

Parallel port – transmits data one byte at a time, with bits travelling simultaneously down a set of wires. This is faster than serial transmission, but not suitable for phone lines. Printers are normally linked through a parallel port.

Serial ports

All computers have one or more serial ports that can be used for getting data into and out of the machine. On a PC there are four, called COM1, COM2, COM3 and COM4. (COM is short for COMunications.)

A port may be a socket at the back of the main case, or reached through an expansion slot inside the case. If your modem is on a card, plugging it into any slot will give it access to the port. You may have to tell it which one.

● Most PC's have a serial port at the back of the machine. This is COM1, and the chances are it has a mouse plugged into it.

● Some PCs have two serial ports on their case. These are COM1 and COM2.

● A few have no external serial ports.

An external modem must, of course, be allocated the port number that it is plugged into; a card modem can be allocated any internal port that is not already in use.

Take note

You will probably find that the modem's pre-set configuration will work with your machine. If it is, you will only have to worry about COM ports when setting up the software.

If you do have to change the COM port, you will also have to change the IRQ (Interrupt ReQuest) setting. See the modem's manual for details.

Buying a modem

❑ A 14,400 or faster model may cost more, but will be cheaper in the end.

❑ If it is Hayes-compatible it will work with almost all comms software.

❑ Be ready to pay a little extra for bundled comms software – but not too much as there is plenty of cheap / free stuff available.

❑ Card modems are easy to install, need no desk space and leave the serial port free.

❑ If you want an external modem, you must have an unused serial port.

❑ Note that you can only legally use BABT approved modems on public phone lines.

Parity and other bits

If you have ever played Chinese whispers, you will know that messages get garbled when you cannot hear clearly. The problem is worse with data communications, for computers cannot guess meanings. Over time a number of different **protocols** have been developed to ensure that data gets through. One of the earliest methods, still in use today, was based on the *parity* bit.

If you look at an **ASCII** table, you will see that the codes for all the normal text characters are less than 128. Now you can represent any numbers from 0 to 127 in binary using only 7 bits. As there are 8 bits to a byte, this leaves one over which can be used for checking purposes – enter the parity bit.

Even parity

With even parity checking, the '1's in each byte are counted, before transmission, and if there are an odd number, the eighth bit is set to '1'. When the byte reaches the other end of the line, if there are not an even number of '1's, the system knows that an error has occurred, and a message is sent out. If the byte gets through intact, the eighth bit is reset to '0' to restore the original character.

Character	ASCII	Binary	Even?	Parity bit set
S	83	01100011	Y	01100011
I	73	01001001	N	11001001
M	77	01001101	Y	01001101
P	80	01100000	Y	01100000
L	76	01001100	N	11001100
E	69	01000101	N	11000101

❏ **Protocol** – set of rules controlling the way that communications are handled. There are many different protocols, so you must ensure that your system and the one at the other end of the line are using the same.

❏ **ASCII** – the American Standard Code for Information Interchange. The most common way of representing characters in a computer system.

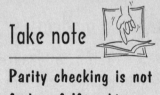

Take note

Parity checking is not foolproof. If two bits are corrupted in the same byte, it will still be even, and the error will not be detected. Parity checking is only the first line of defence against error.

Odd parity

This is the same as even parity, except that the parity bit is adjusted so that every transmitted byte has an odd number of '1' bits. Either method will serve just as well, as long as the systems at both ends of the line use the same one.

Data bits

This refers to the bits in each byte that are used for holding data – typically 7 for ASCII text with parity checking, or 8 for **binary files**.

Stop bits

Some systems mark the end of each character by adding 1, 1.5 or 2 extra bits. (Yes, you can have half a bit as an electrical signal.) The extra bits do increase the length of signal for each character, but if they cut down errors – and retransmissions – then the overall volume of traffic on the line is reduced.

Common Patterns

Parity, data bits and stop bits can be combined in many different ways. The two you are most likely to meet are:

8-N-1   8 Data bits, No Parity and 1 Stop bit.

7-E-1   7 Data bits, Even Parity and 1 Stop bit.

8-N-1 is the most common.

❏ **Binary files** – programs, graphics, sounds, ZIP files and the like. If it isn't simple ASCII text, it's binary. If necessary binary files can be converted to a 7-bit form for transmission over 7 Data bit connections. One of the first Internet tools that you may need, is a decoder to convert these files back to their proper 8-bit form. Don't worry – there are decoders out there, and they are free, and easy to find.

Data transfer protocols

These protocols come into use when you are downloading binary and text files. They control the flow of data, checking for errors and retransmitting corrupted parts of the file. The basic technique is to chop the data flow into blocks, and perform a calculation on the bytes to get a **checksum**. The block and its checksum are then sent off together. The same calculations are performed on the bytes at the other end, and if the result does not agree with the checksum, the receiving system asks for retransmission of that block.

Common data transfer protocols

Kermit   one of the oldest and slowest protocols, but also a reliable one. If all else fails, try Kermit.

Xmodem   another old one, but reliable and in regular use. This works equally well with binary and text files. You will sometimes see it labelled **Xmodem/CRC**. CRC stands for Cyclical Redundancy Check, a mathematically complex, but very effective form of error-checking.

Ymodem   a development of Xmodem, offering slightly faster data transfer.

Zmodem   the main difference here is that Zmodem gives faster throughput and can cope with a total connection failure. With the others, if the line goes down during the transmission of a file, you have to start again from scratch next time you try to download it. With Zmodem, the transfer can pick up where it left off, adding the new data to the part-finished file from the previous session.

Checksums

❏ The simplest technique adds up the values of the bytes, subtracting 256 every time the total goes over that. This results in a single byte checksum. e.g.

Char	Code	Sum
S	83	83
i	105	188
m	109	297
		-256
		41
p	112	153
l	108	261
		-256
		5
e	101	106
Checksum		= 106

Handshaking

Handshaking is used to control the flow of data during the normal run of the session. It is needed because data may well be sent down the line faster than the receiving computer can cope with it.

There are three alternatives:

Hardware   where it is left to the hardware of the systems at both ends.

XON/XOFF   where the handshaking is managed by software. If the computer at the receiving end wants to halt the flow for a moment while it stores received data on disk, it will send an XOFF. An XON restarts the flow.

None   to be used where the other system does not use handshaking. You will rarely meet this.

Software

There are three main types of software that are used for accessing the Internet.

- Basic Communications Software

- Providers' Packages

- Web Browsers and other Winsock aplications

Basic Communications Software

This performs the relatively simple (for software) jobs of controling the modem and the phone, and the interaction with the system at the other end of the line. This is enough to handle e-mail, file transfer and remote working with telnet.

Finding this basic software should not be a problem, nor should it be expensive. You already have suitable software on your system.

- With Windows 95 you have Hyperterminal, a simple but effective terminal emulator program. There are examples of it in action in Section 4, *HyperTerminal*.

- If you have Works or a similar integrated package, you should find a communications module in there.

- There may have been a comms package supplied with your modem. These bundled packages are of varying quality. In general, the older DOS-based ones may be technically very competent, but are rarely as easy to use as newer Windows software.

Tip

The best and simplest thing you can do with HyperTerminal or the freebie that came with your modem, is to use it to make the initial contact with a service and download a decent package of software. Anything else takes time to learn.

Provider Packages

Take note

To access the Web, you need a service provider who can give you an interactive SLIP (Serial Link Interface Protocol) or PPP (Point to Point Protocol) connection to the Internet.

Most service providers offer their own software packages free, or cheap, to their subscribers. Some providers, like CompuServe and WinNET, supply software that is specially written for the service; others supply a set of standard shareware Winsock applications, usually bundled with a program to install it all for you. In either case, they will make working with the service much easier, and are generally worth having.

Web browsers and other Winsock applications

To access the World Wide Web, you need a Winsock. This handles the links and the data transfer between your machine and the remote computers. The most widely used program is Trumpet Winsock, which runs under Windows 3.1 or Windows 95, but Windows 95 also has a built-in Winsock as part of its Dial-Up Networking software. (See page 96.)

Winsock works at the operating system level. If you want to do anything useful with this connection, you need application programs. A Web browser is essential, as is some form of e-mail software. You may also want packages to handle ftp, gopher, news and other on-line work. All are available in shareware, freeware and commercial versions, on the Internet.

Modem commands

With a standard modem, a mainstream service provider, a decent comms package and a bit of luck, you won't have to bother much about these. So, the next couple of pages are for those of you who lack one or more of these, and for those who would like to understand a little more about what the system is doing for them.

Most modems will obey the AT command set. This was developed by the Hayes company and is found in all Hayes-compatible modems. It is a large and comprehensive set, but the few listed on the right will probably be all you ever need. They are used to dial the comms service, initialise the settings, and hang up at the end of the session.

● All start with AT – for ATtention!

● Several commands can be written on the same line.

● Some commands have a symbol (&% or /) before the letter.

Examples:

ATDT 071 284 2424

Dial this number using Tone dial.

AT Q0 V1 \N3 %C3

Typical setup string telling the modem to:

enable verbose error messages (Q0 V1),

use error correction if possible (\N3)

select a suitable compression method (%C3).

AT commands

D Dial, followed by **T** or **P** and the phone number

T Tone dialling (used on all modern exchanges)

P Pulse dialling

H0 or **H** on Hook (Hang-up)

Q0 enable error messages (**Q1** to disable them)

V1 verbose (full text) error messages

&D2 Hang up if DTR signal lost

\N0 no error-correction

\N3 try error-correction, but link anyway if distant modem can't handle it

%C0 no data compression

%C3 automatic selection of V.42bis or MNP data compression

+++ Escape (end session)

Jargon

Carrier Continuous signal to which a second, data signal can be attached. Data Carrier Detect checks that the underlying signal is still present

DCE Data Communications Equipment – the modem

DTE Data Terminal Equipment – a terminal or computer running terminal emulator software

DTR Data Terminal Ready, signal from computer to modem to say that it is ready to receive.

Tip

Always try with the default settings of the modem and your comms software before attempting to set them yourself.

Enable error messages

Error messages as words, not numbers

Turns on Data Carrier Detect when there is an incoming signal

Hang up if there is DTR drop – i.e. the computer-modem link fails

Disable automatic error-correction

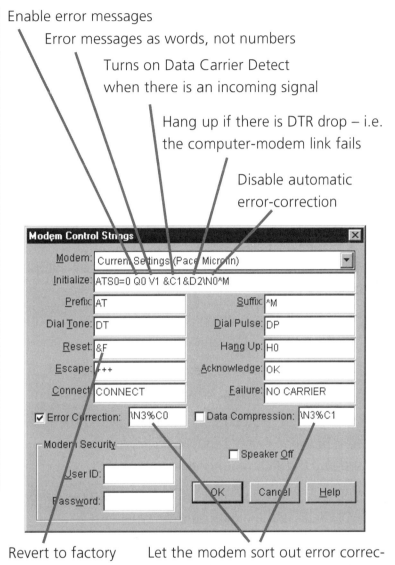

Revert to factory default settings

Let the modem sort out error correction and data compression modes

This screenshot is of the Modem Control Strings dialog box from Compuserve's WinCIM package. Most of these settings were made by selecting the modem from the (long) drop down list in the top slot; only for a few was it necessary to read the modem's manual!

Summary

- **To get on-line**, you need a computer, a modem and a telephone socket. Any type of computer can be used.

- **Modems** may be fitted internally or externally, and must be connected to a COM port. Most will simply plug in and go; some may need configuring to your machine.

- The **Baud rate** describes the speed of a modem. The faster your modem, the lower your phone bills!

- There are different **protocols** that govern the way computers communicate with each other.

- A key protocol covers the number of **data** and **stop bits**, and the type of **parity** used.

- **Parity checking** is a simple but effective way of reducing errors in data transmission.

- Files may be plain **ASCII** text or **binary** – graphics, sounds, programs and other non-text.

- **Data transfer protocols** control the way that files are sent between computers. Xmodem and Zmodem are the two most commonly used.

- You may have to specify the **Handshaking** method. XON/XOFF is the most common type.

- As well as basic **comms software**, you will need additional programs to access the World Wide Web and to make other on-line work simpler. Many service providers offer their own special software packages.

- Most modems are Hayes-compatible, and respond to **AT commands**. You may have to learn a few of these.

44

4 HyperTerminal

Terminal emulation

A normal terminal is a screen and keyboard combination connected to the main computer in a multi-user system. It has no processing power of its own, but sends data and instructions to the main computer for processing.

To connect to some on-line services, your PC must be able to emulate a terminal. There are four main types.

- TTY (TeleTYpe) – handles simple scrolling text only.

- VT-100 – can produce better designed screens, instead of just scrolling text, and can usually interpret some Function key controls .

- VT-52 – also has some screen-handling functions. Rare nowadays.

- ANSI – uses the ANSI codes to handle simple block graphics and colour as well as text.

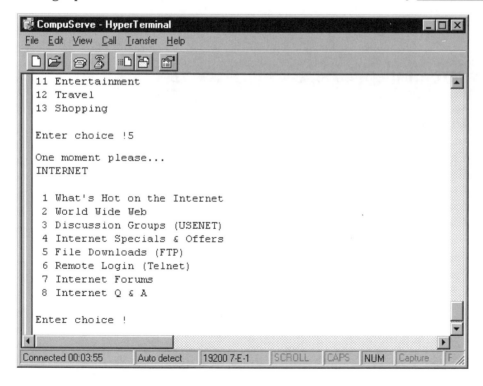

```
CompuServe - HyperTerminal                    _ □ ✕
File  Edit  View  Call  Transfer  Help

11 Entertainment
12 Travel
13 Shopping

Enter choice !5

One moment please...
INTERNET

 1 What's Hot on the Internet
 2 World Wide Web
 3 Discussion Groups (USENET)
 4 Internet Specials & Offers
 5 File Downloads (FTP)
 6 Remote Login (Telnet)
 7 Internet Forums
 8 Internet Q & A

Enter choice !

Connected 00:03:55   Auto detect   19200 7-E-1   SCROLL  CAPS  NUM  Capture  F
```

46

Modem settings

1 From the **Start** menu, point to **Settings** and click **Control Panel**

2 Double click

3 Click the **Properties** button

4 On the **General** panel, check the **COM port** – normally COM 2

5 Set the **Speed** to the fastest the service can cope with – if you can't connect, come back and slow down

6 On the **Connection** panel, set the **Preferences** to suit the service. If in doubt, try **8 - None - 1**

7 Click **OK** and close the Modem dialog box.

The terminal emulation software inWindows 95 is HyperTerminal. Before you start to use it, check the modem settings – through the Control Panel.

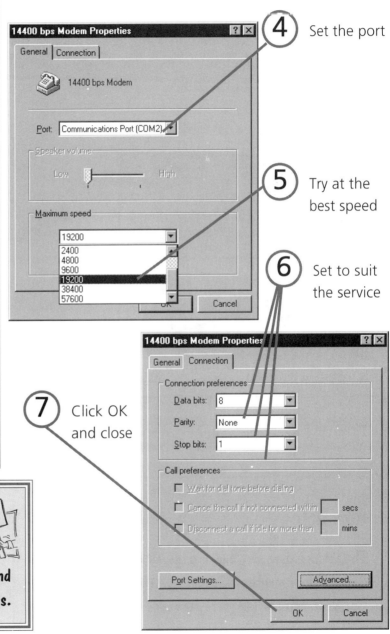

④ Set the port

⑤ Try at the best speed

⑥ Set to suit the service

⑦ Click OK and close

Tip

You can leave Windows 95 to find the best settings for most things.

HyperTerminal

HyperTerminal has a limited but adequate set of tools. Use it to make the initial contact with a service provider, or for occasional link-ups to othersystems. As long as the modem setting are suitable, you should be able to make a connection after filling in two simple panels. These details are saved. Next time you want to connect to the same service, double-click on its icon. HyperTerminal will run, and load in the settings.

Basic steps

1 Run **HyperTerminal**

2 At the **Description** panel enter a filename

3 Choose an icon – some are for specific services, others are general.

4 Click **OK**

5 At the next panel, enter the **Area code** and **Phone number**

6 Check the **Connect using** slot to see that the *modem* is selected

7 Click **OK**

8 At the **Connect** panel, click Dial

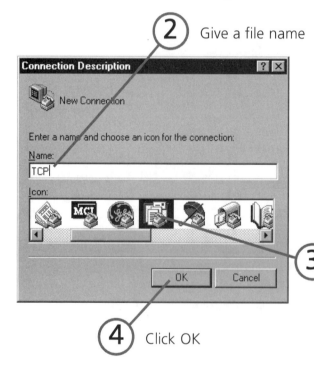

(2) Give a file name

(3) Pick an icon

(4) Click OK

Take note

The settings given here and on page 49 will link you to Total Connectivity Providers. (Section 7.) The initial connection is to Southampton, but there are nodes throughout the UK.

Tip

If HyperTerminal is not on your Start menu, you can find it in the Program Files\Accessories\ HyperTerminal directory.

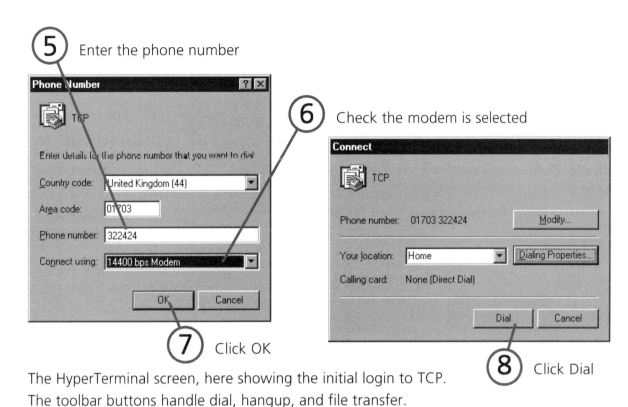

⑤ Enter the phone number

⑥ Check the modem is selected

⑦ Click OK

⑧ Click Dial

The HyperTerminal screen, here showing the initial login to TCP.
The toolbar buttons handle dial, hangup, and file transfer.

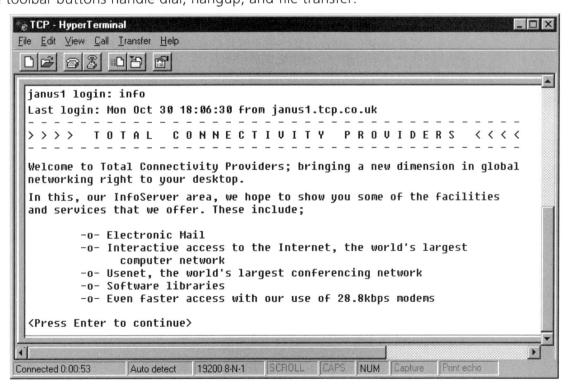

49

Properties

Some properties can only be changed from within HyperTerminal. These properties define how your computer will talk to the one at the other end of the line. Following the rule "if it ain't broke don't fix it", only change those that you know you have to. Leave the rest at their defaults at first. They are probably OK, and can be adjusted later if necessary.

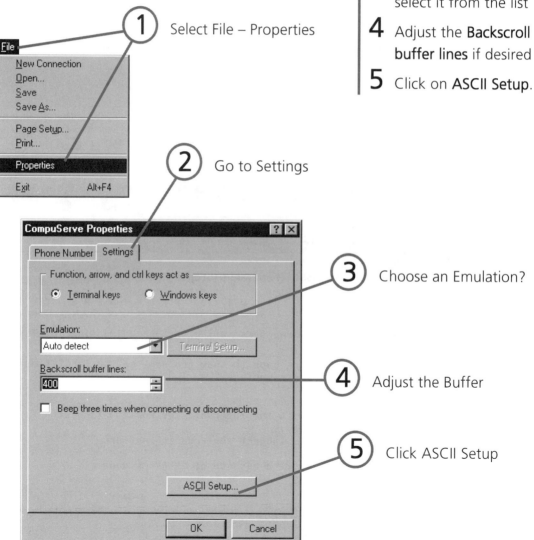

① Select File – Properties

File
New Connection
Open...
Save
Save As...
Page Setup...
Print...
Properties
Exit   Alt+F4

② Go to Settings

CompuServe Properties   ? ☒

Phone Number | Settings

Function, arrow, and ctrl keys act as
  ⦿ Terminal keys   ○ Windows keys

③ Choose an Emulation?

Emulation:
Auto detect ▾   Terminal Setup...

Backscroll buffer lines:
400 ⬍

④ Adjust the Buffer

☐ Beep three times when connecting or disconnecting

⑤ Click ASCII Setup

ASCII Setup...

OK   Cancel

50

Ends of lines

6 If your text is invisible, turn on **Echo typed characters locally**

7 If incoming text overwrites the previous line, turn on **Append line feeds to incoming line ends**

8 Check that the **Wrap** option is turned on

Different types of computers treat ends of lines differently. With some, a line feed doesn't just push the cursor down a line, it also moves it to the left edge of the next. Others need a carriage return to move the cursor to the left.

You may find that lines of incoming text disappear off the right of the screen, rather than wrapping round. Set the **Wrap lines** option to prevent this.

You may get sets of broken lines when you should have paragraphs. Turn off **Append line feeds** setting to fix this. And if the recipients of your messages complain of the same problem, turn off **Send line ends**.

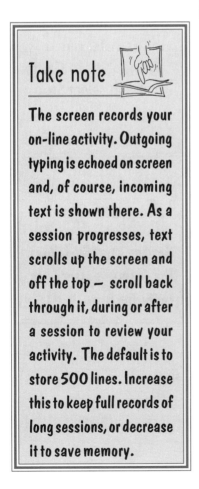

Take note

The screen records your on-line activity. Outgoing typing is echoed on screen and, of course, incoming text is shown there. As a session progresses, text scrolls up the screen and off the top – scroll back through it, during or after a session to review your activity. The default is to store 500 lines. Increase this to keep full records of long sessions, or decrease it to save memory.

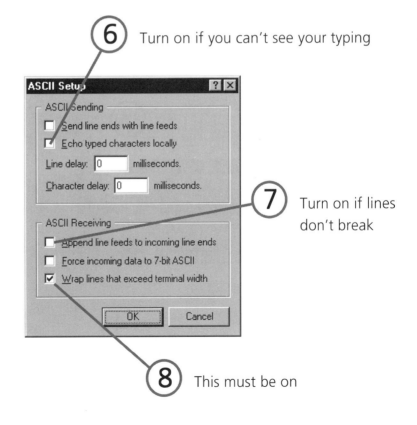

(6) Turn on if you can't see your typing

(7) Turn on if lines don't break

(8) This must be on

Text transfers

Unless you have a very slow connection, text can come down the line faster than you can read it – and it can certainly go out faster than you can type! If you don't need to respond to incoming text immediately, the most efficient way to deal with it, is to save it as a file and read it later. If you have a long message to send, it is best to write it before you go on-line, saving it as a file, then send the file down the line.

● You can capture incoming text as a file, or send a file out at any point during a session.

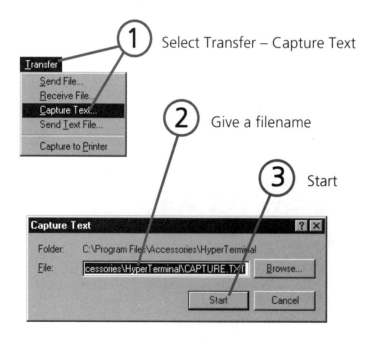

① Select Transfer – Capture Text

② Give a filename

③ Start

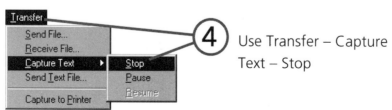

④ Use Transfer – Capture Text – Stop

❑ Setting up

1 Open the **Transfer** menu and select **Capture Text**

2 Type a filename, and path if needed, to replace the default CAPTURE.TXT

3 Click [Start]

4 When you have all the text you want, open the **Transfer** menu again, point to **Capture Text** and select **Stop**

Take note

Sending a text file follows the same pattern as capturing text.

Binary file transfers

1 When you are on-line, find the file you want to download, and select the protocol to be used by the service

2 Select **Transfer – Receive file** or click 🖫

3 Type in a path, or **Browse** for a folder to store the file

4 Select the same **protocol** that you chose at the on-line computer

5 Click ▢ Receive

6 Some protocols pull in the original filename; others prompt you for one

Binary files are those that hold programs, graphics, sounds, and other non-text data. When downloading these you start by selecting the file and the transfer protocol from the on-line computer, then set up your own system to receive it.

● HyperTerminal can use Xmodem, Ymodem, Zmodem and Kermit

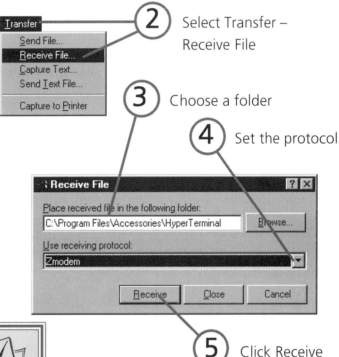

② Select Transfer – Receive File

③ Choose a folder

④ Set the protocol

⑤ Click Receive

⑥ Give a filename if prompted

Summary

❑ **Terminal emulation** makes your PC behave like a terminal attached to a multi-user computer

❑ Before using HyperTerminal, you should check the **Modem** configuration.

❑ **HyperTerminal** is a basic, but adequate terminal emulation program.

❑ When you run HyperTerminal directly, it will take you through the steps for setting up a **New Connection**

❑ With a new connection, try first with the fastest possible **Baud rate**, retrying at a lower speed if necessary.

❑ Not all terminal connections works the same – you may have to adjust the **Properties** to get the best results.

❑ Once you have saved the settings, you can run HyperTerminal from the connection's icon

❑ You can **store incoming text** as a file, and send a file out over the line.

❑ You can **download binary files** via HyperTerminal, using either the Xmodem, Ymodem, Zmodem or Kermit protocols.

❑ When your settings are complete, and saved, use **Phone – Dial** to connect to the service.

5 Compuserve

Making the connection

At the time of writing, CompuServe is the world's largest on-line information service, with over 3 million members. It has been going for over 10 years, and over time has built up a very wide range of information and on-line services. As well as their own extensive in-house services, they also offer access to the World Wide Web and through that to the Internet's newsgroups and other facilities.

You can join CompuServe on a trial basis for a month and see how it fits with your needs. If you would like to do this, either phone for the introductory membership pack (details below), or dial up with your comms software and sign up as shown here. Have your credit card handy – the details are needed for the long term, though if you leave before using up your free time, there will be no charges.

Basic steps

1 Set up a **HyperTerminal** connection with the Settings:

Phone: 0171 490 8881

Terminal: VT100

Communications: 7 Data, Even Parity, 1 Stop bit

Baud Rate: as fast as possible up to 28800

2 Check no-one is using the phone and select **Call – Connect**

3 Wait for the *CONNECT* then press **[Enter]**.

CompuServe introductory membership kit offer

Call **Freephone 0800 289378** or +44 117 976 0680 (from outside the UK), between 9am and 9pm Monday to Friday or 10am to 5pm Saturday, quoting '*Made Simple Special offer, rep number 838*' and state your preference for Windows, Dos or Macintosh software. CompuServe will send you a **free** introductory kit, containing:

- ❑ **CompuServe Information Manager** communications software
- ❑ **Mosaic** Web browser software
- ❑ A **unique ID** and **password** to get you started straight away
- ❑ **Free membership** for **1 month**
- ❑ **10 hours free on-line time** (additional hours charged at £1.95 per hour)
- ❑ **Free subscription** to CompuServe Magazine

All queries relating to this offer should be directed to CompuServe at:

   CompuServe, No 1 Redcliffe Street, PO Box 676, Bristol, BS99 1YN, England, UK

4 At the *prompts* type in these **responses**

Host Name: **CIS**

User ID. **177000,5606**

Password:
   EXPLORE/WORLD

Agreement #:
   MADESIMPLE

Serial Number: **93006**

5 Follow the prompts to register

6 You will be offered a quick tour. Capture the text, so that you can read it at leisure.

❑ If you have any problems, call CompuServe's **Freephone support line**: 0800-289458

Tip

Expect delays between typing and seeing the echo or the next prompt, but if it is more than 15 seconds, you have probably lost the connection. Use Call – Disconnect and start again.

③ Press [Enter]

④ Respond to the prompts

Don't forget the comma

This is not echoed

⑥ Carry on to register

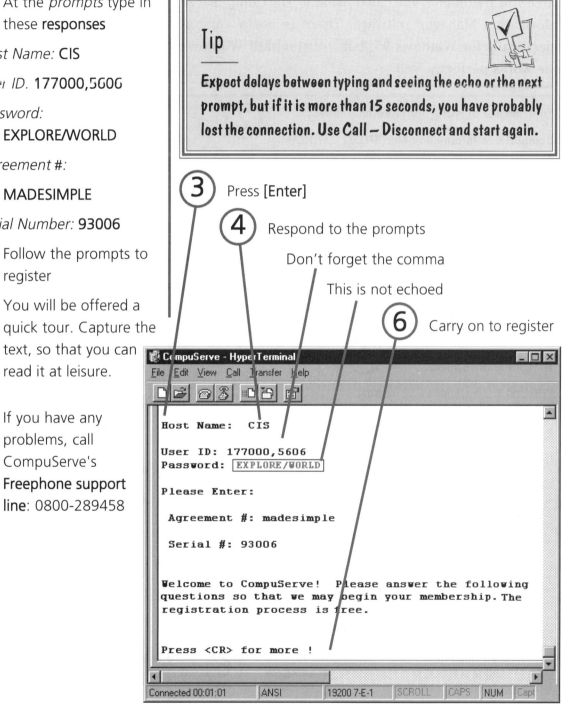

```
Host Name:   CIS

User ID: 177000,5606
Password: EXPLORE/WORLD

Please Enter:

 Agreement #: madesimple

 Serial #: 93006


Welcome to CompuServe!  Please answer the following
questions so that we may begin your membership. The
registration process is free.


Press <CR> for more !
```

Getting CIM

Once you are on-line, you can download the Compuserve Information Manager software. There is not a version specifically for Windows 95, but the standard Windows one works perfectly well.

```
Enter choice or <CR> for more !GO WINCIM

CompuServe Information Mgr(FREE)   WINCIM

 1 Download WinCIM - Complete Program
 2 Download Custom Install of WinCIM
 ...
 7 Order WinCIM
 8 WinCIM Support Forums

Enter choice !1

Complete WinCIM Program(FREE)

 1 Download Complete WinCIM (WCINST.EXE) *4.01MB
 2 Complete Program Installation Instructions

Enter choice !1

WinCIM Downloading:

WINCIM 2.0.1 COMPLETE is free.
You will not be charged for connect time during this download.

Estimated download time:  49:48 minutes

Do you want to download it?(Y/N) y

Transfer protocols available -
1 XMODEM
2 CompuServe B+ and original B
3 DC2/DC4 (capture)
4 YMODEM
5 CompuServe QB (B w/send ahead)
6 Kermit
7 1K XMODEM

Enter choice !1

File name for your computer:  WCINST.EXE

One moment please...
Please initiate XMODEM transfer and press <CR>
when the transfer is complete.
```

1 No matter what else is on screen, you should see the prompt *Enter choice:*

If you are faced with *Press <CR> for more*

keep pressing **[Enter]** (Carriage Return or <CR>) until you get to a *choice* prompt.

2 Type: **GO WINCIM**

3 At the WINCIM menu select the *Complete Program*

4 Select *Download* and confirm the choice

5 You will be prompted for a transfer protocol. From HyperTerminal, XMODEM is the best choice.

6 When you get the *initiate XMODEM transfer* prompt, open the **Transfer** menu and select **Receive File**

7 Follow the Receive File steps on page 53

8 Go and bake a cake while it downloads. Check the progress in the status box from time to time.

9 Press **[Enter]** when it is fully downloaded.

10 Type **exit** to close your connection and **Disconnect** the phone

Select Transfer – Receive File

If the transfer rate (cps = characters per second) drops too low, Cancel and try again later

Check progress

Take note

The WINCIM file is just over 4Mb. At 9600 Baud it will take nearly an hour to download. You may prefer to take the Order option at the WINCIM menu, or ring up the freephone service – the software should arrive in a couple of days.

Setting up

Installation is straightforward – just run SETUP from within Explorer or My Computer, and follow the prompts. This will create a CSERVE folder, along with a set of sub-folders, and copy almost everything into the right place for you. There is one exception...

SETUP will have placed a WINSOCK.DLL file in the \Windows\System folder. *Move this into the CSERVE folder* – it works just as well from there. If you do not, Windows 95 will replace it with its own WINSOCK.DLL at next start-up, and Mosaic will not like that.

Basic steps

1 Open WinCIM , but don't dial up yet.

2 From the **Special** menu, select **Session Settings...**

3 Type in your **Name**, **User ID** and **Password**

4 Set the **Connector** to the right **COM** port

5 Set the **Baud Rate** to the fastest you can, up to 28800.

6 Click **OK**

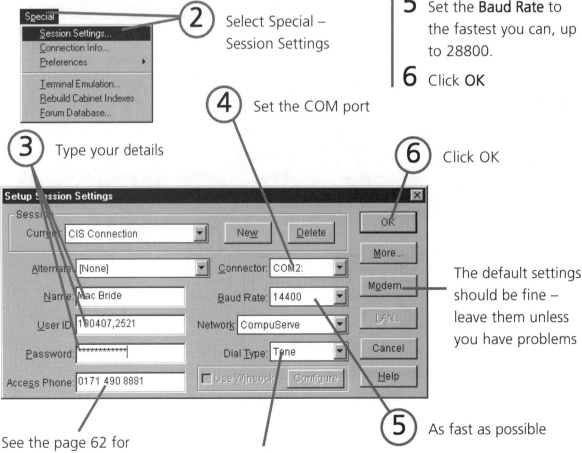

Select Special – Session Settings

Set the COM port

Type your details

Click OK

The default settings should be fine – leave them unless you have problems

As fast as possible

See the page 62 for changing to a local node

Pulse or Tone phone?

Basic steps

Preferences

1 Open the **Special** menu, and select **Preferences**

2 Select a set from the next sub-menu.

3 Set your preferences – largely by clicking check boxes on or off – and **OK** to confirm

Once you have started to work with WinCIM, you may like to adjust the Preferences settings to suit yourself. There is a set of seven, reached through the **Special – Preferences** menu. You can keep coming back to these until you have tweaked it to perfection.

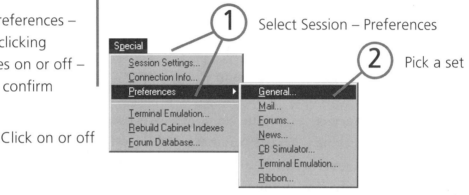

① Select Session – Preferences

② Pick a set

③ Click on or off

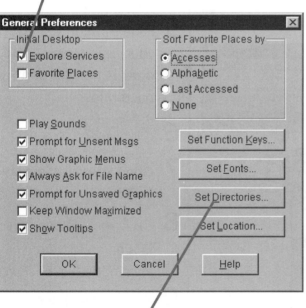

Most of the default directories should be left well alone, though you might prefer to download stuff to your TEMP directory.

Forum logos are pretty, but can be large and slow to download. Turn them off to save time.

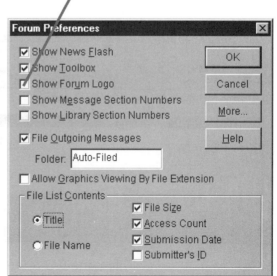

Local nodes

If you live in the UK, your initial connection is to the main node in London, but there is a network of local nodes – as there is in most countries. Check out your nearest. If there is one in your local area and it can handle a high-speed connection, use it rather than the central node. Even if your local node works at a lower Baud rate, it may be worth using this if you spend more time reading or typing on-line than transmitting or receiving data.

Compuserve has a full list of its nodes in every country. They can be reached through the menu sequence: Member Support – Access Telephone Numbers – Access Numbers and Instructions – Access Numbers and Logon Information. The last level is called LGN-10. Knowing this, we can jump straight to it with the GO command.

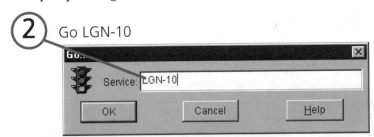

(2) Go LGN-10

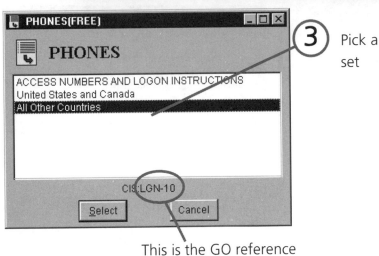

(3) Pick a set

This is the GO reference

1 Click on

2 At the **GO** dialog box, type **LGN-10**. You will be logged on and taken directly to the **PHONES** panel.

3 Select **All other countries**. From here, you are working in the Terminal Emulator.

4 Give the first letter of your country, then select from the list.

5 Page through to find your nearest node, and note its number and baud rates.

6 Click ⎆ to log off

7 Open **Special – Session Settings**

8 Click New and type in a name for your local node

9 Type in the **Phone Number** and set the **Baud Rate** if necessary

10 Click **OK**

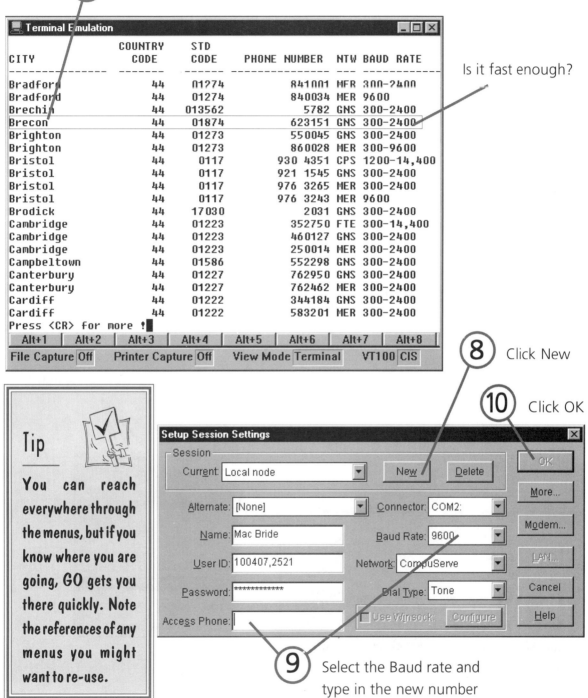

⑤ Note the details of your nearest node

Terminal Emulation

```
              COUNTRY    STD
CITY           CODE      CODE    PHONE NUMBER   NTW BAUD RATE
-------------  -------   ------  ------------   --- -----------
Bradford         44      01274         841001  MER 300-2400
Bradford         44      01274         840034  MER 9600
Brechin          44      013562          5782  GNS 300-2400
Brecon           44      01874         623151  GNS 300-2400
Brighton         44      01273        550045   GNS 300-2400
Brighton         44      01273        860028   MER 300-9600
Bristol          44      0117      930 4351    CPS 1200-14,400
Bristol          44      0117      921 1545    GNS 300-2400
Bristol          44      0117      976 3265    MER 300-2400
Bristol          44      0117      976 3243    MER 9600
Brodick          44      17030          2031   GNS 300-2400
Cambridge        44      01223        352750   FTE 300-14,400
Cambridge        44      01223        460127   GNS 300-2400
Cambridge        44      01223        250014   MER 300-2400
Campbeltown      44      01586        552298   GNS 300-2400
Canterbury       44      01227        762950   GNS 300-2400
Canterbury       44      01227        762462   MER 300-2400
Cardiff          44      01222        344184   GNS 300-2400
Cardiff          44      01222        583201   MER 300-2400
Press <CR> for more !
```

| Alt+1 | Alt+2 | Alt+3 | Alt+4 | Alt+5 | Alt+6 | Alt+7 | Alt+8 |

File Capture Off   Printer Capture Off   View Mode Terminal   VT100 CIS

Is it fast enough?

⑧ Click New

⑩ Click OK

Tip

You can reach everywhere through the menus, but if you know where you are going, GO gets you there quickly. Note the references of any menus you might want to re-use.

Setup Session Settings

Session
Current: Local node   New   Delete

Alternate: [None]   Connector: COM2:
Name: Mac Bride   Baud Rate: 9600
User ID: 100407,2521   Network: CompuServe
Password: ************   Dial Type: Tone
Access Phone: ☐ Use Winsock   Configure

OK
More...
Modem...
LAN...
Cancel
Help

⑨ Select the Baud rate and type in the new number

63

Using WinCIM

CompuServe appreciates that all its members are new sometime, and that many regard it as a tool to be used when needed and not the focus of their life. So, although it does have many sophisticated facilities for dedicated users, it aims to keep things simple. The WinCIM screen is a clear example of their user-friendly approach.

You will find many standard Windows items on the menu bar – **File**, **Edit**, **Window** and **Help** are much the same as in any other package. **Services** and **Mail** are dedicated to the on-line services. Most of the items on these two are duplicated by icons in the toolbar.

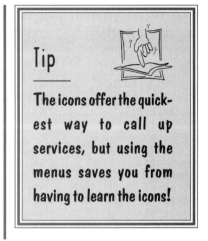

Tip

The icons offer the quickest way to call up services, but using the menus saves you from having to learn the icons!

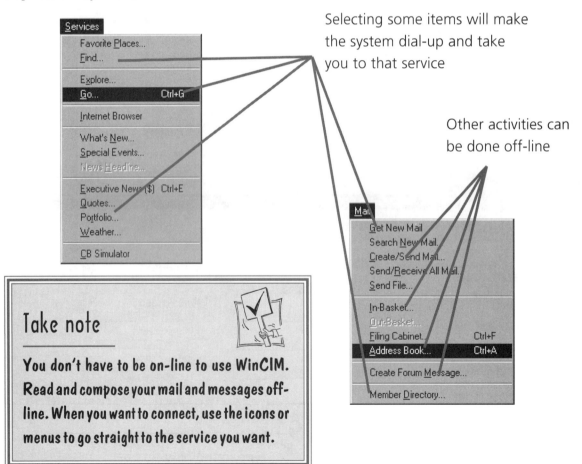

Selecting some items will make the system dial-up and take you to that service

Other activities can be done off-line

Take note

You don't have to be on-line to use WinCIM. Read and compose your mail and messages off-line. When you want to connect, use the icons or menus to go straight to the service you want.

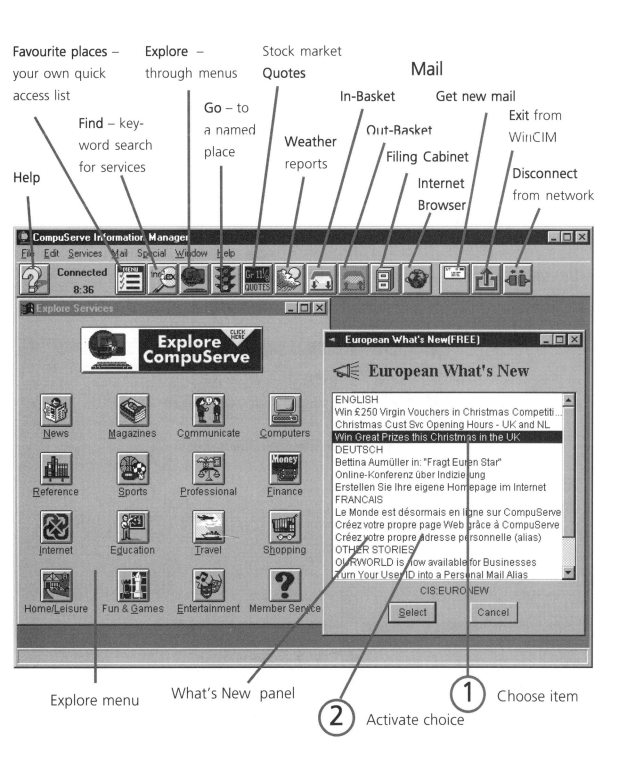

Favourite places –
your own quick
access list

Explore –
through menus

Stock market
Quotes

Mail

Find – key-
word search
for services

Go – to
a named
place

In-Basket

Get new mail

Exit from
WinCIM

Weather
reports

Out-Basket

Filing Cabinet

Disconnect
from network

Help

Internet
Browser

CompuServe Information Manager

File   Edit   Services   Mail   Special   Window   Help

Connected
8:36

MENU

index

Gr 11⅛
QUOTES

Explore Services

Explore
CompuServe

CLICK
HERE

News   Magazines   Communicate   Computers

Reference   Sports   Professional   Finance

Internet   Education   Travel   Shopping

Home/Leisure Fun & Games   Entertainment   Member Service

European What's New(FREE)

European What's New

ENGLISH
Win £250 Virgin Vouchers in Christmas Competiti...
Christmas Cust Svc Opening Hours - UK and NL
Win Great Prizes this Christmas in the UK
DEUTSCH
Bettina Aumüller in: "Fragt Euren Star"
Online-Konferenz über Indizierung
Erstellen Sie Ihre eigene Homepage im Internet
FRANCAIS
Le Monde est désormais en ligne sur CompuServe
Créez votre propre page Web grâce à CompuServe
Créez votre propre adresse personnelle (alias)
OTHER STORIES
OURWORLD is now available for Businesses
Turn Your User ID into a Personal Mail Alias

CIS:EURONEW

Select   Cancel

Explore menu

What's New panel

② Activate choice

① Choose item

Forums

Central to CompuServe is the use of forums – areas for members who share common interests. There are many forums, covering a wide range of interests, hobbies, sports and professional activities. Within each forum there is a Messages area, which serves a similar function to a Usenet newsgroup; a Conference area for on-line discussions; and a Library of files, contributed by its members. As the membership of forums includes many business and professionals, as well as skilled amateurs, some of these libraries are true treasure troves.

Before you can play an active part in any forum, you must join it.

Basic steps

1 Click on an icon in the **Explore** menu.

2 Select a general area of interest from the top-level menu.

3 Highlight a forum in the list.

4 Click Select

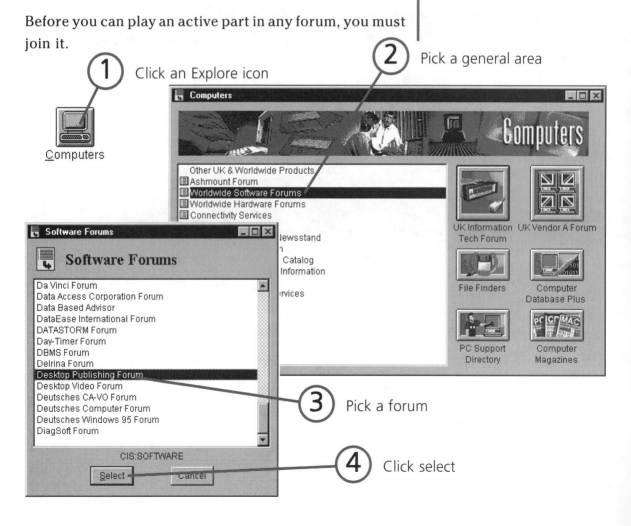

① Click an Explore icon

② Pick a general area

③ Pick a forum

④ Click select

Go...

Service: internet

OK   Cancel   Help

Exit forum

Forum toolbox

Public message board for sharing ideas

Store of files for downloading

On-line chats with other members

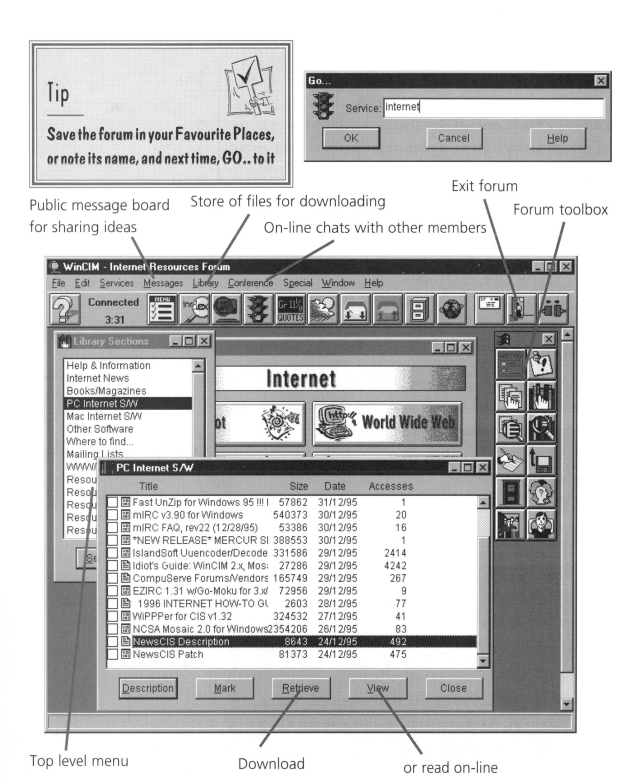

WinCIM - Internet Resources Forum

File   Edit   Services   Messages   Library   Conference   Special   Window   Help

Connected 3:31

Library Sections

Help & Information
Internet News
Books/Magazines
PC Internet S/W
Mac Internet S/W
Other Software
Where to find...
Mailing Lists
WWW/
Resou
Reso
Resou
Resou
Resou

Internet

World Wide Web

PC Internet S/W

	Title	Size	Date	Accesses
	Fast UnZip for Windows 95 !!! I	57862	31/12/95	1
	mIRC v3.90 for Windows	540373	30/12/95	20
	mIRC FAQ, rev22 (12/28/95)	53386	30/12/95	16
	NEW RELEASE MERCUR SI	388553	30/12/95	1
	IslandSoft Uuencoder/Decode	331586	29/12/95	2414
	Idiot's Guide: WinCIM 2.x, Mos:	27286	29/12/95	4242
	CompuServe Forums/Vendors	165749	29/12/95	267
	EZIRC 1.31 w/Go-Moku for 3.x/	72956	29/12/95	9
	1996 INTERNET HOW-TO GL	2603	28/12/95	77
	WiPPPer for CIS v1.32	324532	27/12/95	41
	NCSA Mosaic 2.0 for Windows	2354206	26/12/95	83
	NewsCIS Description	8643	24/12/95	492
	NewsCIS Patch	81373	24/12/95	475

Description   Mark   Retrieve   View   Close

Top level menu

Download

or read on-line

67

File finder

If you are looking for a particular file, and don't want to have to hunt through forum libraries for it, try File Finder. You don't even have to know the file's name – though that helps. You can search CompuServe's databases using any one or a combination of:

- Keyword
- Submission date
- Forum
- File Type e.g. ASCII, binary
- Extension e.g. EXE, ZIP, COM, TXT
- File name
- Submitter

Wildcards can be used, just as they can in MSDOS and Windows, with * standing for unknown characters. In the example, we are looking for PKZIP, the file compression program, using this :

PKZIP*.*

This will find anything that starts with PKZIP, whatever else the name includes, and whatever the extension. In fact, it turns up several versions of PKZIP and the Frequently Asked Questions text on it.

Tip

Two other files are well worth finding and downloading: PKUNZIP.EXE, the uncompressor, and WNMAIL26.ZIP, the program to use with WinNet – see the next section.

Basic steps

1. Jump to PC File flnder with **GO pcff**
2. Select **Access File Finder**
3. At the next panel, choose your search criteria, e.g. **File Name** and give what detail you can
4. Start the search
5. The panel shows how many files have been found, and has a new **Display** option – select it
6. Select a file from the **Display** list
7. Click Retrieve to download
8. Close the panels to return to the top menu, or disconnect with 

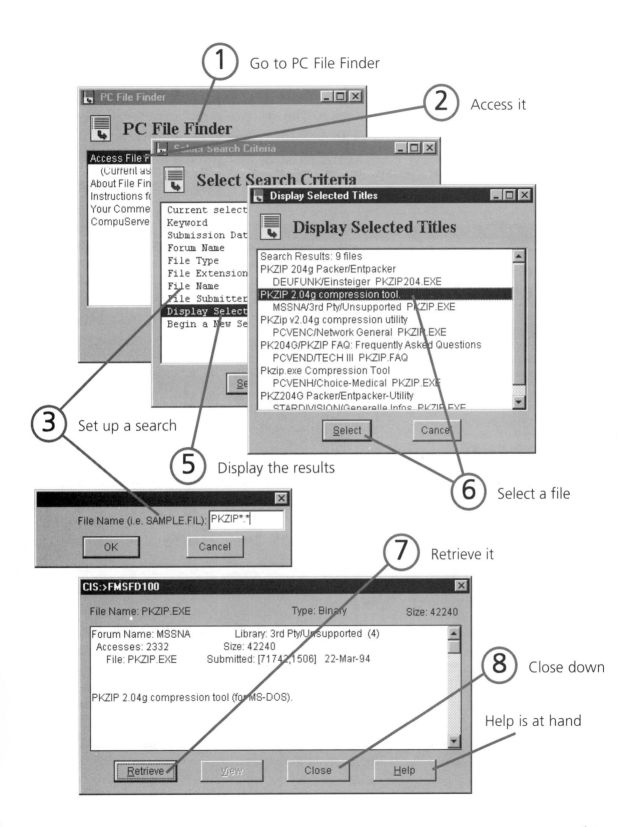

① Go to PC File Finder

② Access it

③ Set up a search

⑤ Display the results

⑥ Select a file

⑦ Retrieve it

⑧ Close down

Help is at hand

PC File Finder

Access File F
(Current as
About File Fin
Instructions fo
Your Comme
CompuServe

Select Search Criteria

Current select
Keyword
Submission Dat
Forum Name
File Type
File Extension
File Name
File Submitter
Display Select
Begin a New Se

Display Selected Titles

Search Results: 9 files
PKZIP 204g Packer/Entpacker
    DEUFUNK/Einsteiger PKZIP204.EXE
PKZIP 2.04g compression tool.
    MSSNA/3rd Pty/Unsupported PKZIP.EXE
PKZip v2.04g compression utility
    PCVENC/Network General PKZIP.EXE
PK204G/PKZIP FAQ: Frequently Asked Questions
    PCVEND/TECH III PKZIP.FAQ
Pkzip.exe Compression Tool
    PCVENH/Choice-Medical PKZIP.EXE
PKZ204G Packer/Entpacker-Utility
    STARDIVISION/Generelle Infos PKZIP.EXE

Select   Cancel

File Name (i.e. SAMPLE.FIL): PKZIP*.*

OK   Cancel

CIS:>FMSFD100

File Name: PKZIP.EXE   Type: Binary   Size: 42240

Forum Name: MSSNA   Library: 3rd Pty/Unsupported (4)
  Accesses: 2332   Size: 42240
    File: PKZIP.EXE   Submitted: [71742,1506] 22-Mar-94

PKZIP 2.04g compression tool (for MS-DOS).

Retrieve   View   Close   Help

Go ftp

ftp – file transfer protocol – is the tool that allows you to get files from host machines on the Internet. The system is set up for the normal *anonymous* login, with your address (*User ID@compuserve.com*) as the password.

❑ Getting there
1 Go ftp

either if you know the URL

2 Access a **Specific Site**

3 Type the site name and the directory

or browse

4 Select **Popular Sites**

5 Pick a site from the list

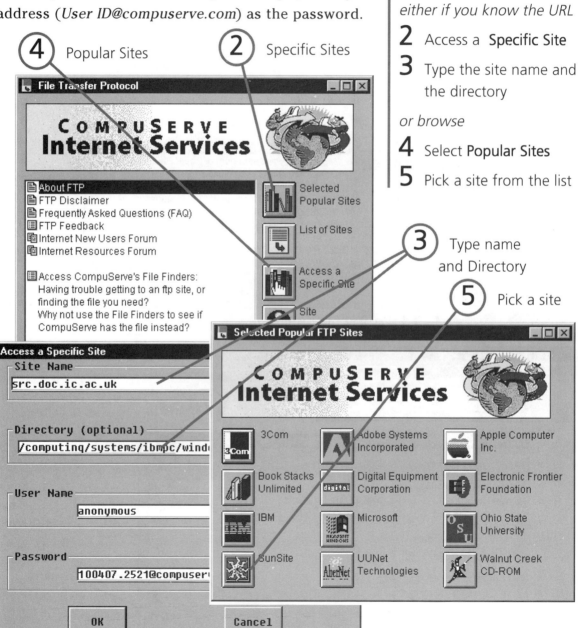

Basic steps

Working on-site

1 Change directories if necessary

2 Select and View any README file

3 Select and Retrieve the file you want

4 Repeat for any other files then Leave

If you have got the URL, you can get the file. Even if you haven't got a URL, you can browse to see what's available.

Take note

Copies of many of the most popular files are stored on Compuserve's computers. Take the strain off the Internet connections and download from Compuserve if you can. To check their files, GO filefinder.

---

(1) Set the Directory

(2) View README

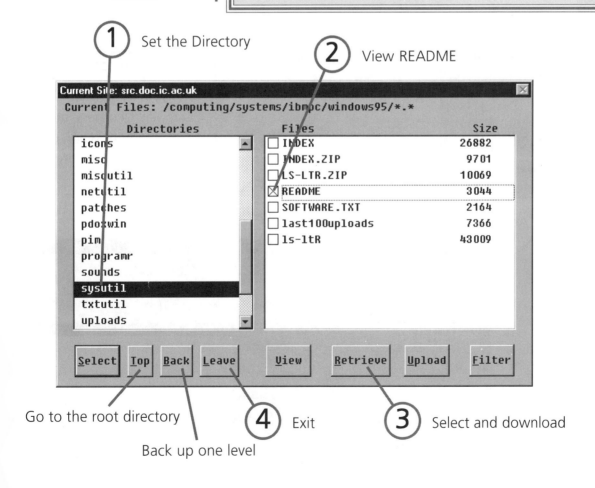

Current Site: src.doc.ic.ac.uk

Current Files: /computing/systems/ibmpc/windows95/*.*

Directories	Files	Size
icons	☐ INDEX	26882
misc	☐ INDEX.ZIP	9701
miscutil	☐ LS-LTR.ZIP	10069
netutil	☒ README	3044
patches	☐ SOFTWARE.TXT	2164
pdoxwin	☐ last100uploads	7366
pim	☐ ls-ltR	43009
programr		
sounds		
sysutil		
txtutil		
uploads		

Select | Top | Back | Leave | View | Retrieve | Upload | Filter

Go to the root directory

(4) Exit

(3) Select and download

Back up one level

71

Communications

Creating Mail

Mail can be composed and read either off- or on-line. You will probably find that it is simplest to scan incoming mail and reply to brief notes while on-line, but to deal with longer ones after you have logged off.

WinCIM has its own editor for creating mail, but you can, if you prefer, write your messages in your favourite word-processor, save them as text files, and then send the files through the mail system.

1 Select **Create Mail...** from the **Mail** menu

2 If the recipient is in your **Address Book**, select the name and ⌐Copy >>⌐ it into the **Recipient** list,

otherwise

3 Type in the **Name** and e-mail **Address**, select an **Address Type** and click ⌐<< Copy⌐ to add to your Address Book

4 If you want to send copies to others, add their names when **CC** is highlighted

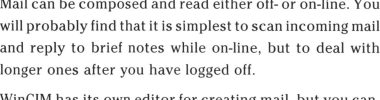

(1) Select **Mail – Create/Send Mail**

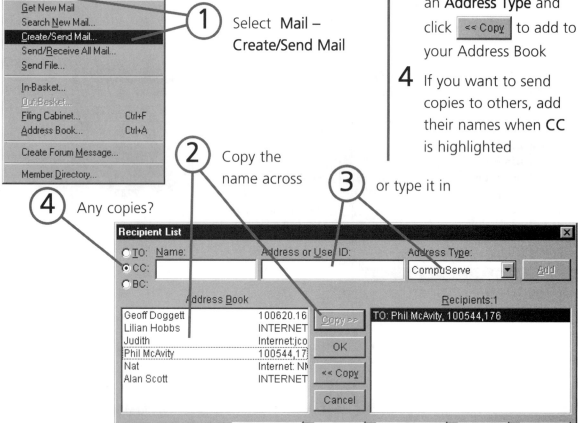

(2) Copy the name across

(3) or type it in

(4) Any copies?

72

Names and Addresses

5 Click **OK**

6 Type a **Subject** line – this alerts the recipient to the content of the mail (see next page)

7 Type your message, using the usual WIndows techniques to edit it.

8 Click Send Now – the system will log you on, if you are off-line, and send it.

Names are for human use, so write these to suit yourself; **Addresses** are for the e-mail system, and must be exact.

● If the recipient is another Compuserve member, all you need is the User ID. For Phil McAvity, in the example, the address is 100544,176

● If the recipient is elsewhere on the Internet, the address must start with *INTERNET:* and have the full *name@domain* address, e.g.

  INTERNET:macbride@macdesign.win-uk.net

⑥ Type the Subject ...

⑦ .. and the message

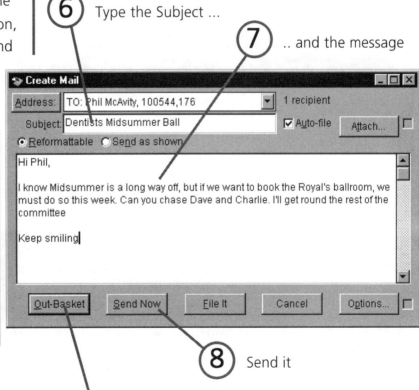

Tip

CompuServe's communications services include classified ads and a CB simulator as well as mail.

⑧ Send it

If you have several messages to write, pile them up in the Out-Basket and use Mail – Send/Receive All Mail when you get on-line

Getting mail

Incoming messages are stored in your mailbox at CompuServe. If there are any, you will see a **mail messages waiting** prompt when you log in. Use **Send/Receive all mail** to get them. (Set the **Preferences – Mail** to *Delete Retrieved Messages*, to delete them from your mailbox.)

After reading your messages, either delete them or file them on your own machine. Other options in the reading window allow you to reply, or to forward the mail to a third party – perhaps after adding some comments.

Basic steps

1 Open the **Mail** menu and select **Send/ Receive all Mail**

2 Scan the subject lines to see what the messages are about

3 Open a message

4 Read you new mail and deal with it

> **Tip**
>
> Check your mailbox regularly. If you let it clog up with old mail you will start to incur storage charges.

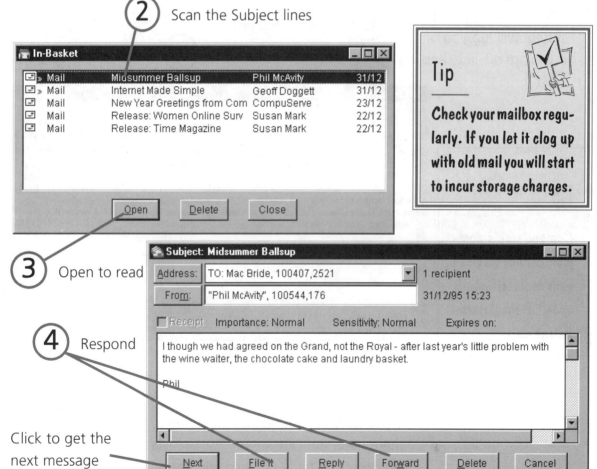

② Scan the Subject lines

Open to read

Respond

Click to get the next message

Other services

Before we leave CompuServe, it is worth mentioning the other services offered to its members.

News

Fun & Games

Reference

Finance

Shopping

Travel

- News gives access to PA News Online, Reuter UK News Clips and many other worldwide newswires.

- Games covers multi-user on-line games – keep the kids off these! – as well as libraries of games for downloading.

- Reference materials are drawn from over 850 databases including on-line versions of some major reference works and an Encyclopedia.

- Finance covers stock market quotes, sources of advice for investors, insurance and other financial services.

- In the on-line Shopping centre you can buy hardware, software, books, flowers, chocolates, and much else besides.

- Travel links you to the worldwide airline booking system so that you can plan your travel arrangements, and even book tickets. (Though your local travel agent can probably do you a better deal!) The new UK accommodation and travel section includes railway timetables, AA Roadwatch, restaurants and golf club guides.

- Magazines, health, education, reviews of films, videos, plays and books....and much more

Take note

CompuServe now offers access to the World Wide Web, and provides its own browser. (See page 122)

Summary

❑ You can **try CompuServe for free** with the Made Simple special offer!

❑ The **CompuServe Information Manager** can be downloaded, or sent for by snail mail. It will need a little configuration before you first use it.

❑ CompuServe has **local nodes** throughout the country. You may find it cheaper and easier to connect to one of these, rather than the London main node.

❑ In **WinCIM**, you can access services through the icons or by selecting from menus.

❑ There are **forums** to cover most interests and many occupations. As a forum member you have access to the forum's libraries of files and can comunicate with other members, either by mail or in on-line conferences.

❑ The **File finder** facility lets you track down files from ConpuServe's databanks.

❑ If you can't find what you want in File finder, you can use **ftp** to download files from anywhere in the Internet.

❑ **E-mail** can be composed and read on- or off-line.

❑ CompuServe offers **other information services** to its members, as well as Internet access.

6 WinNET

Starting with WinNET

WinNET is the e-mail and Usenet News service of the PC User Group, and if what you want from the Internet is mail and news, it is probably the simplest and most effective solution around today. What makes it so easy to use are two excellent Windows software packages - WinNET Mail and WinTools.

Getting the software

Either download the software using Terminal, as shown here, or ring the PC User Group. (See the panel.)

You will have to register with them to use the service. This can also be done either by e-mail or voice phone. When registering, please state that you are an Internet Made Simple reader. Your first month's membership will cost you less than this book, and give you a chance to judge how far WinNET suits your needs.

1 Open **HyperTerminal** and make the **Settings**:

Phone: 0181 723 7300

Communications: 8 Data, No Parity, 1 Stop bit

Baud Rate: up to 28800

2 Select **Call – Connect**

3 For the *nickname*, type **WINNET**

4 For the *password*, press **[Enter]**

5 Type **1** for the **Download** menu

6 At *--More --* press the **[Spacebar]**

7 At the second list, select WNMAIL26.ZIP. (The latest may be 27, 28 or higher when you read this.)

8 Select Zmodem – this protocol picks up the filename and retrieves the file automatically

9 Download WNTOOLS.ZIP in the same way.

The PC User Group

can be contacted at:

PO Box 360, 84-88 Pinner Rd
Harrow HA1 4LQ, England
Tel: +44 (0)181-863 1191
Fax: +44 (0)181-863 6095
E-Mail: help@win-uk.net

The mail service costs £6.75 + VAT per month.
The group also offers an interactive service, with full World Wide Web connection, for £8.25 + VAT

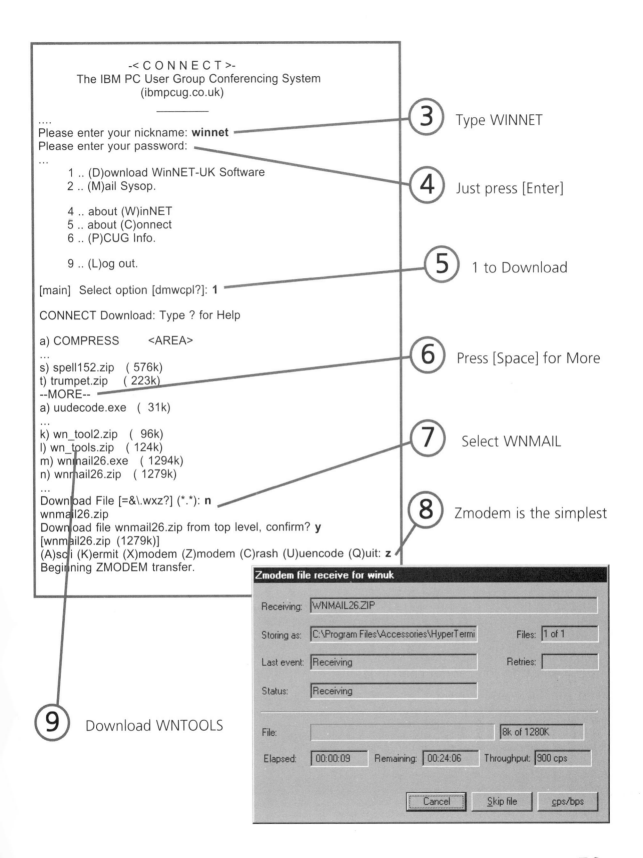

```
              -< C O N N E C T >-
        The IBM PC User Group Conferencing System
                  (ibmpcug.co.uk)
                  _____
....
Please enter your nickname: winnet
Please enter your password:
...
      1 .. (D)ownload WinNET-UK Software
      2 .. (M)ail Sysop.

      4 .. about (W)inNET
      5 .. about (C)onnect
      6 .. (P)CUG Info.

      9 .. (L)og out.

[main]  Select option [dmwcpl?]: 1

CONNECT Download: Type ? for Help

a) COMPRESS        <AREA>
...
s) spell152.zip  ( 576k)
t) trumpet.zip   ( 223k)
--MORE--
a) uudecode.exe  ( 31k)
...
k) wn_tool2.zip  ( 96k)
l) wn_tools.zip  ( 124k)
m) wnmail26.exe  ( 1294k)
n) wnmail26.zip  ( 1279k)
...
Download File [=&\.wxz?] (*.*): n
wnmail26.zip
Download file wnmail26.zip from top level, confirm? y
[wnmail26.zip (1279k)]
(A)scii (K)ermit (X)modem (Z)modem (C)rash (U)uencode (Q)uit: z
Beginning ZMODEM transfer.
```

(3) Type WINNET

(4) Just press [Enter]

(5) 1 to Download

(6) Press [Space] for More

(7) Select WNMAIL

(8) Zmodem is the simplest

(9) Download WNTOOLS

Zmodem file receive for winuk

Receiving: WNMAIL26.ZIP

Storing as: C:\Program Files\Accessories\HyperTermi   Files: 1 of 1

Last event: Receiving   Retries:

Status: Receiving

File: 8k of 1280K

Elapsed: 00:00:09   Remaining: 00:24:06   Throughput: 900 cps

Cancel   Skip file   cps/bps

Setting up

Unzip wnmail into a temporary folder and run SETUP.EXE. Unzip wn_tools into another folder (e.g. \TEMP\TOOLS) and then run its SETUP program from there.

When installing the **program files**, just let it run through on the default settings – it knows what it's doing. The **System Names** and **Communications** parameters do need some input from you.

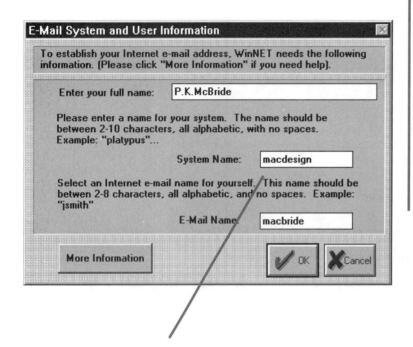

Think carefully about this. The system name is the only one you cannot change later.

System Names

Three names are required:

❑ Your normal **full name**;

❑ a **system** name of between 2 and 10 characters to identify your domain;

❑ an **e-mail** name of between 3 and 8 characters

System and e-mail names should be letters or digits only – no spaces – and are combined to form your e-mail address, in the form:

email@system.win-uk.net

Notes

Communications

❑ The **Phone number** can include your Mercury code if appropriate

❑ The **Interface speed** can be set higher than your modem's baud rate, as compression pushes the effective rate up.

❑ Set the **CPU utilization** to Medium or High to begin with. You can adjust it later, when you have seen how it works in practice.

You should be familiar with most of what you see here – with one exception. The Call Server program (see next page) runs in the background – i.e. you can be doing other things while it gets your mail. The system needs to know how much priority to give to this. With very high **CPU utilization**, when Call Server is running, any other active programs will almost grind to a halt, but you will get your mail downloaded and filed on disk quickly. Set to low, the Call Server's activities will scarcely interrupt your other work.

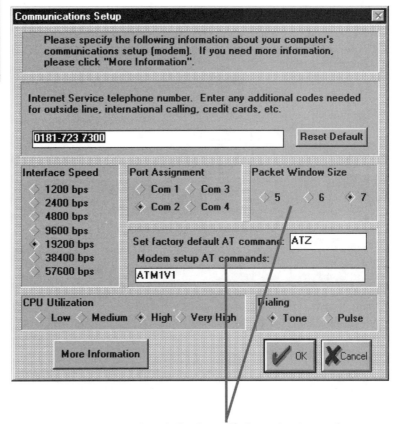

Communications Setup

Please specify the following information about your computer's communications setup (modem). If you need more information, please click "More Information".

Internet Service telephone number. Enter any additional codes needed for outside line, international calling, credit cards, etc.

`0181-723 7300`   **Reset Default**

Interface Speed
◇ 1200 bps
◇ 2400 bps
◇ 4800 bps
◇ 9600 bps
◆ 19200 bps
◇ 38400 bps
◇ 57600 bps

Port Assignment
◇ Com 1 ◇ Com 3
◆ Com 2 ◇ Com 4

Packet Window Size
◇ 5   ◇ 6   ◆ 7

Set factory default AT command: `ATZ`
Modem setup AT commands:
`ATM1V1`

CPU Utilization
◇ Low ◇ Medium ◆ High ◇ Very High

Dialing
◆ Tone ◇ Pulse

More Information   ✔ OK   ✗ Cancel

Leave the defaults – if they don't work, you can run Setup again and adjust them

Take note

WinNET has local dial-in nodes throughout the UK, as well as the main nodes in London. If you would prefer to connect to one of these, use the Select Node option of WinTools. (See page 85.)

Off-line mail

WinNET is an off-line system. You call up, once a day, to pick up your mail and news, and to send any messages you have written. If you subscribe to half a dozen or so newsgroups, and have a moderate amount of mail, your connect time should be no more than a minute or two.

The whole process is automated. All you have to do is set the Call Server running. It then sends and receives all the files, hangs up the phone, and stores the mail and newsgroup articles in the appropriate places.

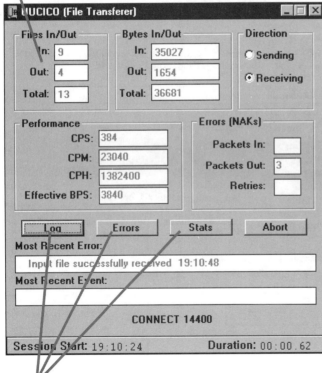

(2) Watch files come and go

Log, Error reports or Usage Stats can be obtained from Call Server, while it is running, or from WinTools

1 Run  Call Server from the Start menu, or click

    in WinMail, or

    Call Server in WinTools.

2 Restore it from its Taskbar icon and watch it while it runs, or go for a cuppa

❑ As Call Server closes down, it sets MainMan running, to sort the post. When this has finished, you will see a **New Mail** icon at the bottom of your screen.

3 Double click the **New Mail** icon to open up WinNET mail.

4 Read your mail.

Print current mail

Run Call Server

Reply to current mail

Open incoming mail folder

Forward to third party

Open Newsgroup list

Open mail folder list

Move message to
another folder

Tidy display

Write new mail

Delete   Work through list

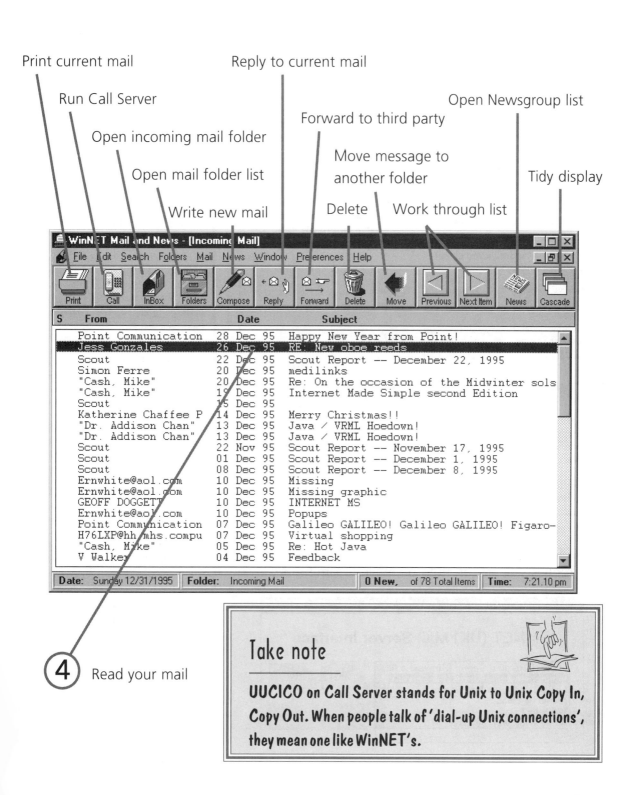

④ Read your mail

Take note

UUCICO on Call Server stands for Unix to Unix Copy In,
Copy Out. When people talk of 'dial-up Unix connections',
they mean one like WinNET's.

WinNET tools

This neat little utility gives simple access to the suite of programs that make up the WinNET system. Some of these can also be accessed directly from Program Manager (or the Start menu in Windows 95); some cannot be reached any other way.

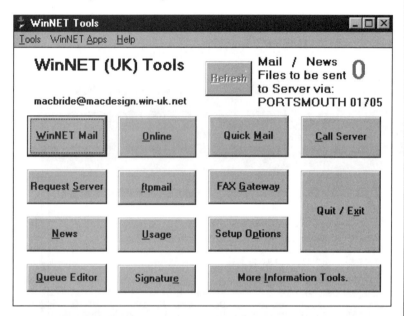

Use **Request Server** to get files, interrogate the Movie Database (a must for fans), or change your Mail List subscriptions. Each option has a dialog box for creating your requests. They can then be mailed from here.

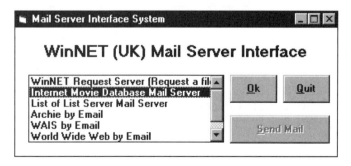

Queue Editor lets you into the queue of messages waiting to be sent, to view or delete them. You cannot *edit* messages in the queue.

FAX Gateway links to your phone/fax system to send a file as a fax.

Quick Mail is for brief messages, perhaps with files attached.

Usage opens a sub-menu with:

Log Files accesses the same error reports, usage log and stats that you see in Call Server. It also lets you delete old log files.

Server Stats sends a request to WinNET to let you know how much time you have used, and what you owe them.

Setup Options leads to a sub-menu, which includes the option **Select Node** Use this to switch to a node near you.

With **Signature** you can create a short text file to add to all your mail as your personal signature. Signatures often include witty quotes or ASCII 'art' – pictures created with characters. Netiquette requires that it should be no more than 4 lines long.

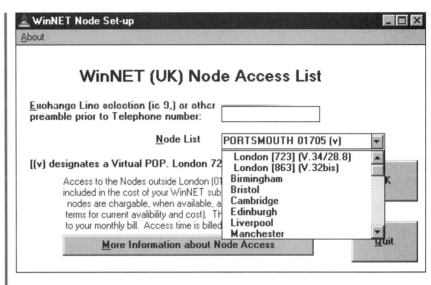

The Daemon dialler

To run Call Server automatically every day, go to the Setup Options and use **Scheduler** to set the dial-up times, then go to the Taskbar Settings and add DAEMON.EXE to your Startup folder

Take note

Any tools not covered here are deal with in the next few pages.

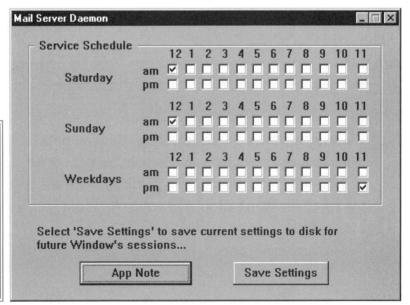

Newsgroup subscription

WinNET's system makes subscribing to newsgroups very simple. All you have to do is pick your group and tell the system you want to subscribe. It will mail a subscription request to the appropriate place and set up a **folder** to store incoming articles. When you join a newsgroup, you normally start to receive articles the next day.

Unsubscribing is done in much the same way. Note that when you leave a group, its articles generally continue to come through for a few days. These are collected in the **News not subscribed to** folder.

```
┌─ Usenet News Group Folders ──────────── _ □ ✕ ┐
│ #New      News Group Name                       │
│┌───────────────────────────────────────────────┐│
││   46    comp.internet.net-happenings           ││
││  173    comp.unix.questions                    ││
││   12    connect.chatter                        ││
││   24    news.not.subscribed.to                 ││
││    3    rec.arts.books                         ││
││   17    rec.humor.funny                        ││
││   39    uk.comp.os.win95                       ││
││                                                ││
│└───────────────────────────────────────────────┘│
└──────────────────────────────────────────────────┘
```

opens the **News Group Folder** list. Clicking on a folder name then opens it. The numbers in the list show how many new (unread) articles there are in each folder. Some groups generate far more articles than others.

Basic steps

❑ Subscribing

1 Open WinTools and select [**News**] then
   [**News Subscription**]

2 Drop down the list of **Which News Group** categories

3 Pick a category and click [**Search**]

4 Scroll through the resulting list to see what's there.

5 If you find a group that looks interesting, select it and click [**Subscribe**]

6 Repeat steps 2 to 5 as wanted, then **Quit**.

❑ Your subscription requests will be posted next time you use Call Server.

❑ Unsubscribing

1 Select the group from the list on the right

2 Click [**Unsubscribe**]

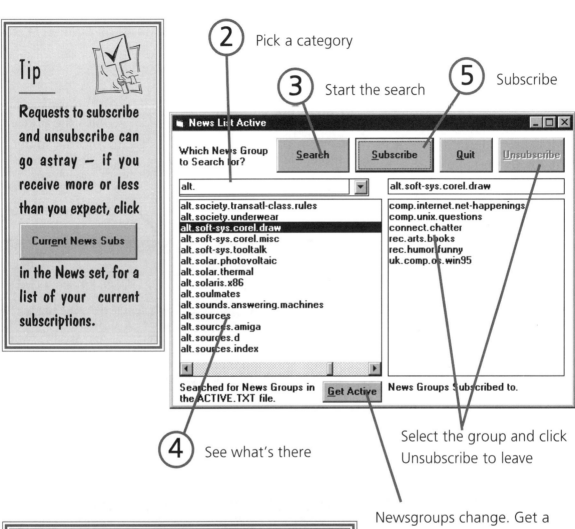

② Pick a category

③ Start the search

⑤ Subscribe

News List Active

Which News Group to Search for?   Search   Subscribe   Quit   Unsubscribe

alt.

alt.soft-sys.corel.draw

alt.society.transatl-class.rules
alt.society.underwear
alt.soft-sys.corel.draw
alt.soft-sys.corel.misc
alt.soft-sys.tooltalk
alt.solar.photovoltaic
alt.solar.thermal
alt.solaris.x86
alt.soulmates
alt.sounds.answering.machines
alt.sources
alt.sources.amiga
alt.sources.d
alt.sources.index

comp.internet.net-happenings
comp.unix.questions
connect.chatter
rec.arts.books
rec.humor.funny
uk.comp.os.win95

Searched for News Groups in the ACTIVE.TXT file.   Get Active   News Groups Subscribed to.

④ See what's there

Select the group and click Unsubscribe to leave

Newsgroups change. Get a new list of Active groups from WinNET every few months.

The news desk

If people are using the Subject line properly, you can see at a glance whether or not you want to read the article. Having read it, you can respond in several ways.

Submit an article – be relevant and brief

Copies the article into your editor, tacking **Re:** to the subject line. Edit it and add comments, before posting.

Copies the article to another folder, where it will not be deleted when you do a cleanup.

Print a copy on paper

Respond to author only

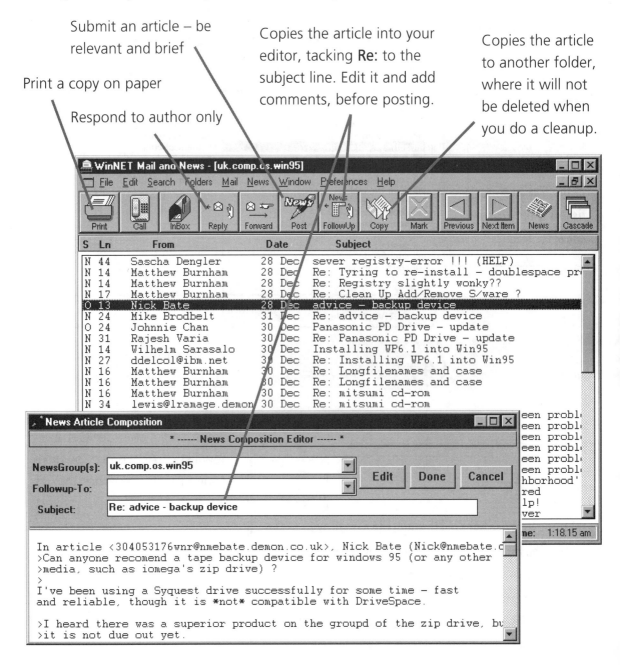

Basic steps

1 Run Cleanup , or
select | **News** | then
| **News Cleanup** | in
WinTools

2 Set the age limit for
the cleanup.

3 Decide whether you
want **Cleanup** and/or
Archive

4 Click | **START** |

If there are a lot of old
articles to shift, go and
have a cup of tea.

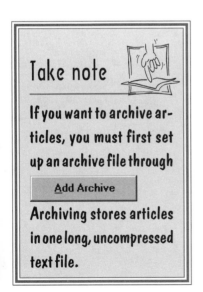

Take note

If you want to archive articles, you must first set
up an archive file through

| **Add Archive** |

Archiving stores articles
in one long, uncompressed
text file.

Cleaning up

One of the problems of belonging to newsgroups is the
amount of storage space required. The half dozen groups
that I subscribe to, generate a Megabyte of files each
week – and only one of these has heavy traffic. Join
alt.tv.xfiles or *alt.startrek* (one of 12 Star Trek newsgroups)
or any other group that attracts large numbers of articu-
late enthusiasts, and you will soon be wondering where
all your hard disk went. Fortunately there is a Cleanup
program that removes old articles.

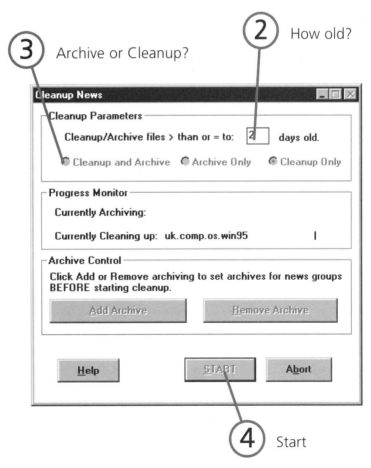

③ Archive or Cleanup?

② How old?

④ Start

Summary

- **WinNET** is an off-line mail-based service run by the PC Users Group.

- The Group also offers an **interactive SLIP connection**, for Web access.

- WinNET **Mail** and **Tools** are efficient and well-designed programs that make it easy to get the best out of the system.

- The **Call Server** can be set to run automatically at a chosen time each day, or you can call up as and when you need to.

- You can access the USENET and other **newsgroups** through WinNET.

- There are simple facilities for subscribing to newsgroups, and for archiving or removing old news articles.

7 Winsock

Local links to the World

CompuServe and the PC User Group are only two of the many organisations, large and small, providing access to the Internet. The smaller firms initially served only their local area, though an increasing number now also have a national network of nodes. Small providers can sometimes be an excellent choice, offering a more personal service and high level of support, but the quality is variable. Growth rates are high, and not all firms expand their hardware and phone connections fast enough. Trying to get on-line through such a firm can be frustrating.

TCP (Total Connectivity Providers) is an example of a small service which can be reached through a national network of nodes. It provides full and easy access to the World Wide Web, interactive ftp (for getting files), archie (for finding them), plus an e-mail system – all in Windows packages. The programs they supply are all standard shareware or freeware. All TCP does is what any good service should do – they configure the software so that it is ready for you to use, and they bundle it into one neat, self-installing package.

1 Contact TCP (details below) and sign up. They will set up your account and send you a disk and brief manual.

2 When you get the disk, go into Windows and run the INSTALL program from File Manager. You will need about 3.5 Mb of disk space.

3 Accept their suggestions at the prompts and in a few minutes you will have a new program group.

Take note

TCP more commonly stands for Transfer Control Protocol and is the basis of interactive access over the Internet.

Free Trial Offer

Mention 'The Internet Made Simple' when you join and TCP will waive the initial set-up fees, and give you one month's free trial subscription.

TCP is at: PO Box 454, Southampton, SO16 3WR

Tel: 01703-393392
E-mail: sales@tcp.co.uk

Basic steps

1 Run the **TCP** program

2 Open the **File** menu and select **Setup**.

3 Type in the IP address of your server

4 The **SLIP port** is your COM port – 1 or 2

5 Set the **Baud rate**

6 Check **Internal SLIP**, **Hardware Handshake** and **Van Jacobson compression**

7 Click **OK**

Trumpet Winsock works well and may be easier to set up than the Windows 95 version of Winsock. Once installed, it needs to know the IP address of your name server, as well as basic modem details.

Take note

When you install Trumpet Winsock, you must move the **WINSOCK.DLL** file out of the \Windows\System folder. Windows 95 automatically restores its own **WINSOCK.DLL** file into this folder at the start of day. Place Trumpet's **DLL** in the folder containing your comms applications.

(3) Type Name Server address

(2) Select File – Setup

```
File
 Setup
 Register
 Firewall Setup
 PPP options
 Exit
```

(4) Set port

(5) Set Baud rate

Some services give users fixed IP addresses, others allocate them at login

(6) Check these

(7) Exit

Network Configuration

IP address	193.130.249.143
Netmask	0.0.0.0
Name server	193.132.77.1 158.4
Domain Suffix	tcp.co.uk

Default Gateway 0.0.0.0
Time server

Packet vector 00   MTU 1006   TCP RWIN 3018   TCP MSS 966
Demand Load Timeout (secs) 5   TCP RTO MAX 60

☑ Internal SLIP   ☐ Internal PPP

SLIP Port 2
Baud Rate 19200
☑ Hardware Handshake
☑ Van Jacobson CSLIP compression

Online Status Detection
○ None
● DCD (RLSD) check
○ DSR check

Ok   Cancel

Logging in

Whichever of the applications – ftp, e-mail or web browser – you want to use, you must first run Winsock and login to your service. Winsock can then be minimised out of the way until you have finished your session.

On the latest versions of Winsock, the first time you login you will be prompted for the phone number, your user name and password. After this, the login script will run automatically.

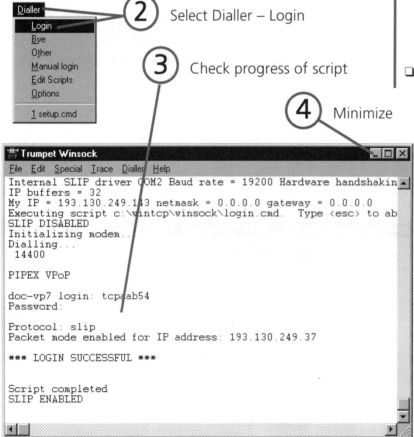

Select Dialler – Login

Check progress of script

Minimize

Don't forget about Winsock! When you have finished browsing, or whatever, restore the window and use **Dialler – Bye** to close down the connection.

Basic steps

1 Run **TCP** (Winsock)

2 Open the **Dialler** menu and select **Login**

3 Watch the script run through and make sure all is well.

4 Once you have the **Script completed** message, click the **Minimize** button.

❑ You are ready to run an application.

Tip

If you don't get through – because of a poor line, or the service is busy – press [Esc], wait a moment and try again.

Basic steps

1 Select **Dialler – Edit Scripts**

2 Open **login.cmd**. This will take you into Notepad for editing.

3 Replace:

<telno> with the your provider's number.

<name> with your user name. It will probably need **-slip** or **-pop** at the end – check your paperwork.

<password> with the password you have been given.

4 Save and exit back to Winsock.

Tip

If you change to an alternative phone number, you will have to edit the phone entry in your **TRUMPWSK.INI** file – it's right at the bottom.

Editing the Login script

With earlier versions of Winsock you have to edit the login script to give it the phone number, your ID and password.

● If no basic script has been provided, follow the pattern shown here, and save it as *login.cmd*.

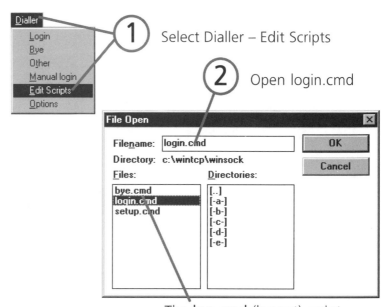

Select Dialler – Edit Scripts

Open login.cmd

The **bye.cmd** (logout) script normally reads: sleep 3
output +++
sleep 3
output ath0\r

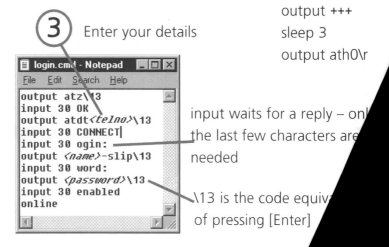

Enter your details

input waits for a reply – on the last few characters are needed

\13 is the code equiv of pressing [Enter]

Dial-Up Networking

If you want to use the Windows 95 Winsock and have not installed Dial-up networking, open the Control Panel and use Add/Remove Programs to do so now.

There are two aspects to configuring a new connection:

- the network software within your computer

- the connection to the service provider.

1 Open the **Control Panel** and select **Network**

2 Click **Add**

3 Select **Protocol** and click **Add**

4 Select **Microsoft** and **TCP/IP**, then click **OK**

5 Select the TCP/IP entry, click **Properties**

6 Work through the tabs

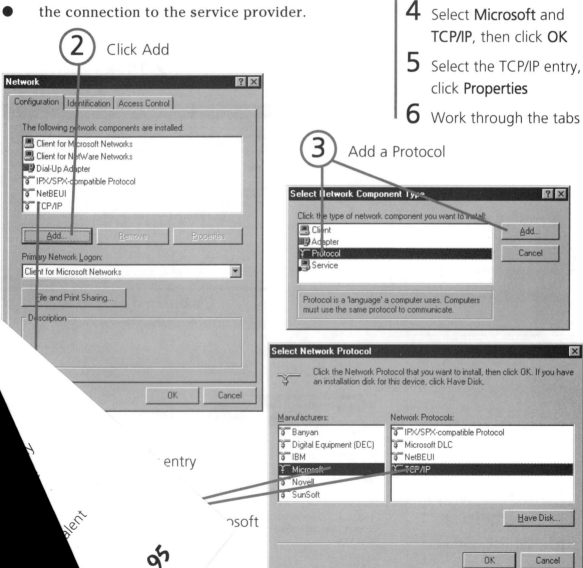

② Click Add

③ Add a Protocol

Network ? X

Configuration | Identification | Access Control

The following network components are installed:

- Client for Microsoft Networks
- Client for NetWare Networks
- Dial-Up Adapter
- IPX/SPX-compatible Protocol
- NetBEUI
- TCP/IP

[Add...] [Remove] [Properties]

Primary Network Logon:

Client for Microsoft Networks ▼

[File and Print Sharing...]

Description

[OK] [Cancel]

Select Network Component Type ? X

Click the type of network component you want to install:

- Client
- Adapter
- Protocol
- Service

[Add...] [Cancel]

Protocol is a 'language' a computer uses. Computers must use the same protocol to communicate.

Select Network Protocol X

Click the Network Protocol that you want to install, then click OK. If you have an installation disk for this device, click Have Disk.

Manufacturers:	Network Protocols:
Banyan	IPX/SPX-compatible Protocol
Digital Equipment (DEC)	Microsoft DLC
IBM	NetBEUI
Microsoft	TCP/IP
Novell
SunSoft

[Have Disk...]

[OK] [Cancel]

entry

soft

95

IP address: select
Obtain IP address automatically

WINS Configuration: select *Disable WINS resolution*

Advanced: select *Set this protocol as default*

Bindings: check *Client for Microsoft networks*

Configuration A

Gateway: leave it blank

DNS Configuration: select *Disable DNS*

Configuration B

Gateway: type in the address

DNS Configuration: type your e-mail name as the *Host*, your provider's name as the *Domain*, and ADD their IP address as the *Primary DNS*

Windows 95 is new, and service providers are still adapting to it. I've come across two approaches – one specifies the servers at this point, the other does it in the Dial-Up configuration. Either way you must know your provider's DNS addresses.

6 Work through the tabs

A Disable DNS and leave Gateway blank

B Enter DNS and Gateway details

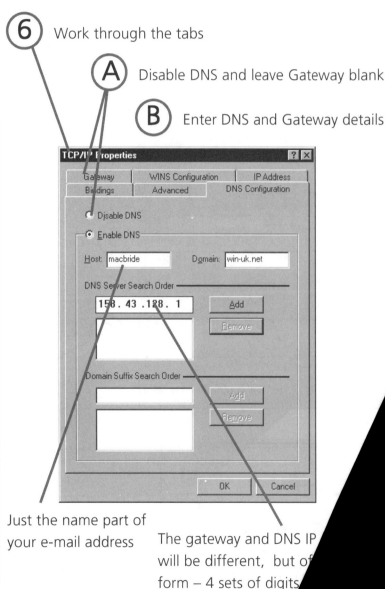

Just the name part of your e-mail address

The gateway and DNS IP will be different, but of form – 4 sets of digits

The Dial-Up connection

Once the Network software is in place, you can set up the connection. A Wizard handles the donkey work, leaving it to you to set the Properties.

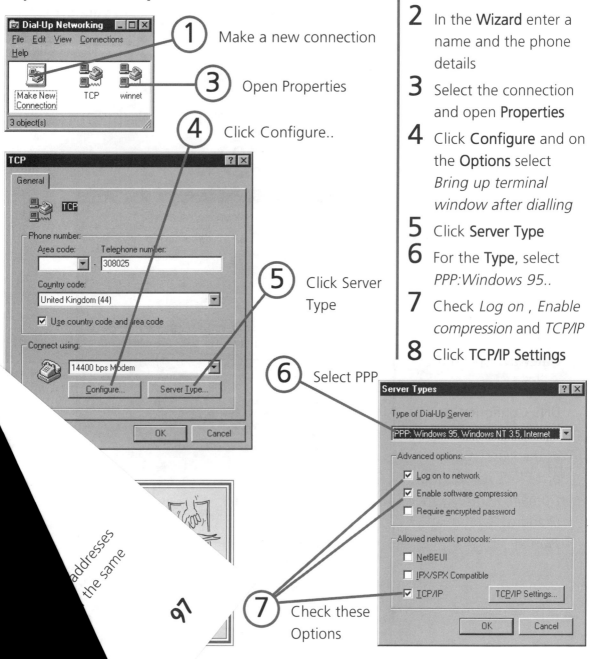

① Make a new connection

③ Open Properties

④ Click Configure..

⑤ Click Server Type

⑥ Select PPP

⑦ Check these Options

Basic steps

1 Open the **Dial-Up** folder and click **Make New Connection**

2 In the **Wizard** enter a name and the phone details

3 Select the connection and open **Properties**

4 Click **Configure** and on the **Options** select *Bring up terminal window after dialling*

5 Click **Server Type**

6 For the **Type**, select *PPP:Windows 95..*

7 Check *Log on* , *Enable compression* and *TCP/IP*

8 Click **TCP/IP Settings**

9 Set **Server assigned IP address**

A WIth Configuration A set **Specify name server** and enter the addresses

B With configuration B set **Server assigned name server address**

❑ **Logging in**

1 Double click the connection's icon

2 Click **Connect**

3 At the Terminal Screen, enter your *user name*, *password* and *PPP* when prompted.

4 After the *Packet mode enabled* (and some garbage), click **Continue**

❑ Run your applications

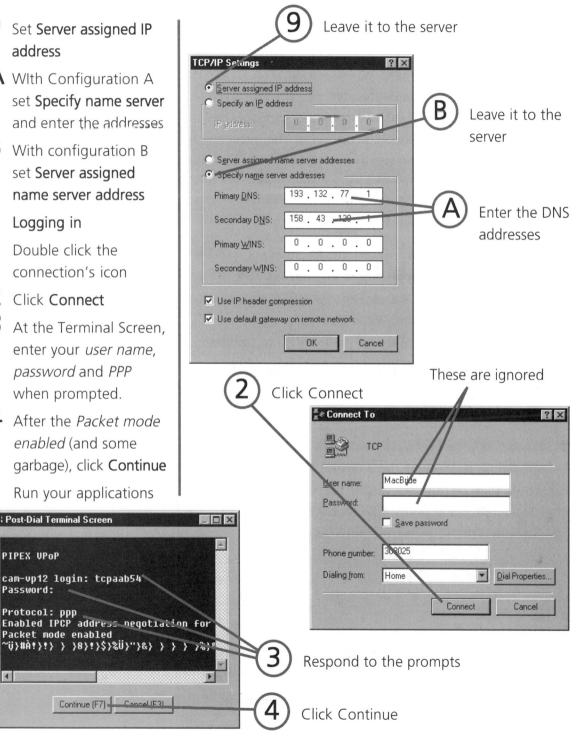

⑨ Leave it to the server

Ⓑ Leave it to the server

Ⓐ Enter the DNS addresses

These are ignored

② Click Connect

③ Respond to the prompts

④ Click Continue

Archie file locator

You can use ftp to browse through remote databanks to see what's there, but it's a slow way to find files. Far better to get Archie to track them down for you. To use it, you have to connect to an Archie server – preferably your nearest – and give it part of, or the whole, name of the file you want to find. The Archie program at the server will then search the Internet's archives and come up with the URL's (locations and names) of matching files.

Substring searches

It is quite likely that you will not know the exact name of the file. For example, if you may come across MPEG files – videos for computers – and want an MPEG program to play them on your system. What will the program file be called? It is a fair bet that it will have MPEG in the name.

- Don't use wildcards. This is not DOS. Give the bit you know (or guess). If there is a file that contains it anywhere in the name, it will be matched.

- Do be as complete as you can. The shorter the substring, the longer the search. Archie estimated it would take 30 minutes to find all matches for 'MPEG' – I aborted at that point! Specifying 'MPEGWIN' instead cut down the search time substantially.

Take note

Giving the exact name makes the search simpler and quicker. Restricting the search to a domain also speeds things up. If an exact, restricted search fails, you can try a wider one later.

Basic steps

1 Use Winsock to login.

2 Run **Archie**.

3 Enter the name – or part of the name – of the file to **Search** for.

4 Click **Exact** if you gave the whole name; **Substring**, if you gave only a part.

5 Select an **Archie server** from the list, trying the closest first.

6 If you want to restrict the search to the UK, type *uk* in the **Domain** slot.

7 Click Search to start.

8 Give it a moment to locate the host, then check the **Status Bar**.

9 If there is a long **Queue** of other users, click Abort , select a new server and try again there.

❑ If you are successful, you will see a list of file details.

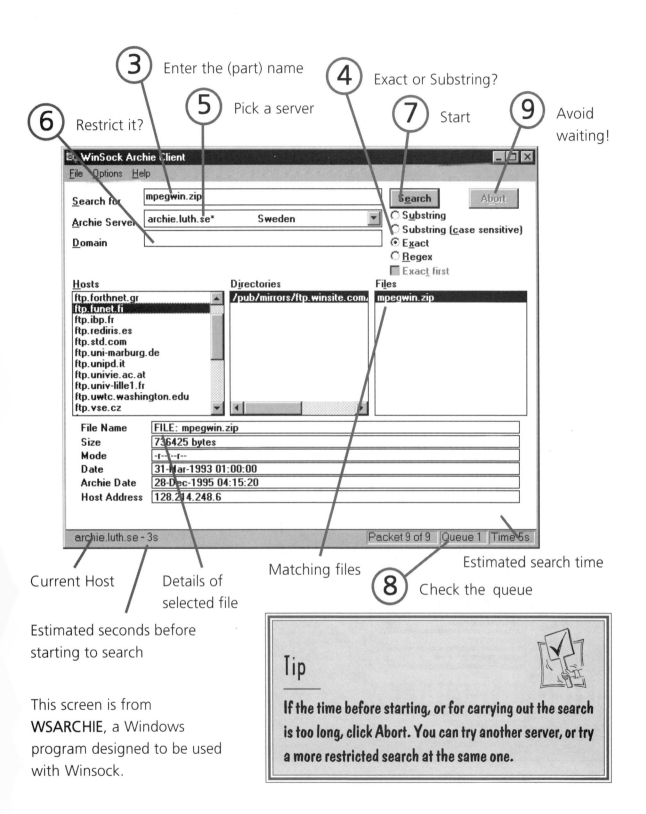

(3) Enter the (part) name

(5) Pick a server

(4) Exact or Substring?

(7) Start

(9) Avoid waiting!

(6) Restrict it?

WinSock Archie Client

File Options Help

Search for   mpegwin.zip

Archie Server   archie.luth.se*   Sweden

Domain

- ○ Substring
- ○ Substring (case sensitive)
- ⦿ Exact
- ○ Regex
- ☐ Exact first

Search   Abort

Hosts
ftp.forthnet.gr
ftp.funet.fi
ftp.ibp.fr
ftp.rediris.es
ftp.std.com
ftp.uni-marburg.de
ftp.unipd.it
ftp.univie.ac.at
ftp.univ-lille1.fr
ftp.uwtc.washington.edu
ftp.vse.cz

Directories
/pub/mirrors/ftp.winsite.com/

Files
mpegwin.zip

File Name	FILE: mpegwin.zip
Size	736425 bytes
Mode	-r--r--
Date	31-Mar-1993 01:00:00
Archie Date	28-Dec-1995 04:15:20
Host Address	128.214.248.6

archie.luth.se - 3s

Packet 9 of 9   Queue 1   Time 5s

Matching files

Estimated search time

(8) Check the queue

Current Host

Details of selected file

Estimated seconds before starting to search

This screen is from **WSARCHIE**, a Windows program designed to be used with Winsock.

> ## Tip
>
> **If the time before starting, or for carrying out the search is too long, click Abort. You can try another server, or try a more restricted search at the same one.**

ftp the easy way

WS_FTP.EXE is a Windows program for use with Winsock, and offers probably the simplest way to do ftp. You tell it where you want to go, and what directory to start at, then send it off to make the connection. A few points to note:

● You must login through Winsock first.

● You must know exactly the host name.

● If you know the path to the directory, it speeds things up. If you do not give it, you will start at the top of the directory structure and have to work your way down.

● You won't always get through – the site may be off-line, or already crowded with other ftp'ers. Try later.

● All ftp URL references take the form:
  ftp://host.name/path/to/directory/filename
  Use the information to set up your connection.

1 Run FTP

2 Pull down the **Profile** list and pick a site

or

Create a profile for a new site. Click **New** and enter a profile name and the exact **Host name**.

3 Make sure that **Anonymous login** in checked. This sets the **User ID** to *Anonymous* and the **Password** to your user ID.

4 Enter the directory path on the **Remote Host**, if known.

5 Click **Save** if you have set up a new profile, or made changes that you want to keep.

6 Click **OK** to start the connection.

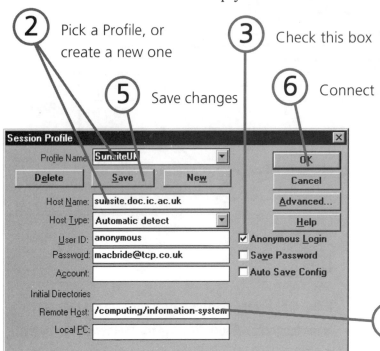

② Pick a Profile, or create a new one

③ Check this box

⑤ Save changes

⑥ Connect

④ Set the Directory

Basic steps

1 Change directory if need be – use the same techniques as in any File Manager

2 Highlight a file that interests you

3 Opt for **ASCII** to transfer text files, **Binary** for any others

4 Set the directory on your local system to receive a file

5 Click ⌐ to download

6 Use ⌐ Close ⌐ to return to the first panel and set up a new session

7 Click ⌐ Exit ⌐ to end

Using the ftp connection

Ftp gives you a two-way, interactive connection to the remote host. You can treat its directories and files as if they were in a drive in your own machine – almost.

● Downloading is like copying a file from another disk – but much slower. Be patient.

● If you want to upload a file, only do so into a directory that welcomes contributions – if you can't see one called UPLOADS, they probably don't want your files.

● Don't delete or edit files or directories on the Host – it shouldn't let you, but it might have let its guard slip.

● View any README or similar files . They can be useful.

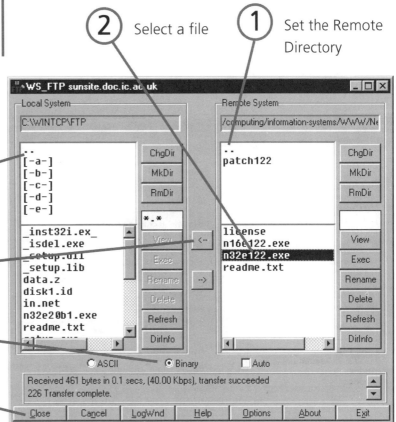

② Select a file

① Set the Remote Directory

④ Set the Local Directory

⑤ Download

③ ASCII or Binary

⑥ New host

Gopher it

HGOPHER is a freeware Windows gopher program for Winsock users. As gophering is tending to become a specialist ocupation, gopher software is not always supplied by service providers.

Some configuration is usually necessary. Gopher items include text, graphics and sounds files, and it needs to know what software to use to view them. It will have found some viewers on installation; others you must tell it about. The list can be added to at any time, as needed.

Basic steps

1 Start Winsock, but don't login, and run **Gopher**

2 Select **Options – Viewer Set up**.

3 In the **Select View type** list, pick one that can be viewed on your system.

4 If **Viewer** is empty, type in the path and filename ending with **%f**, (to stand for the name of the data file) then click Accept

5 Repeat 3 and 4 for all the types you can use, then click Done

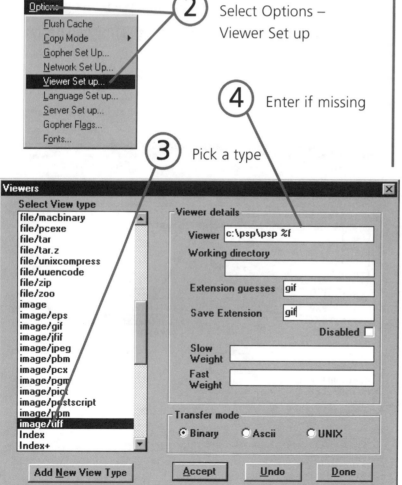

② Select Options – Viewer Set up

④ Enter if missing

③ Pick a type

Take note

As Gopher does a good job of installing itself, you should find that many of the viewers are already set up correctly

104

Basic steps

Gophering

1 Login through Winsock and run Gopher.

2 Open the **Commands** menu and select **Go Home**, to take you to your gopher server.

3 Click on an item name to select it. This will take you to another menu or run a viewer so that you can read/ view/hear the file.

4 To save items for future reference, open the **Commands** menu and select **Save As**

All you really need to know to start exploring gopherspace, is that clicking a menu item's name selects that item. Finding the parts that interest you is another matter – but just keep following the trails through the menus. They will take you there.

● When you find sites that you want to return to in future, add them to your **Bookmark** list and you will be able to jump straight to them next time.

● As you gain experience, you might like to investigate the **Options** to tweak the screen displays and your interaction with gopher.

Click for information on the item

Click on the name to select

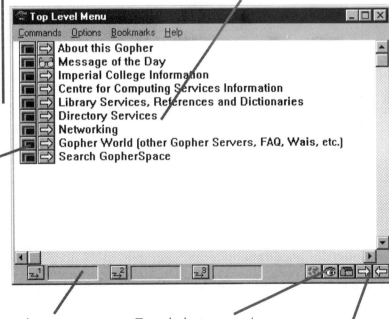

You can have up to three open links at a time. Counters show the progress of incoming data.

Toggle between view and file-saving modes

Backwards and forwards through open menus

Eudora mail

This is a freeware Winsock mail program, that can be used on- or off-line. It offers no Help, but is straightforward to use. There is a comprehensive set of commands and a small but sufficient set of icons. Customising is simple, with a clearly laid out configuration dialog box, and a set of check box switches to cover most options.

One of Eudora's attractive features is its simple means of attaching text or binary files to messages for transmission through the mail.

1 If the network configuration has not been done by your suppliers, get the details from them.

2 Open the **Special** menu and select **Configuration**.

3 Fill in the **Network configuration** details if necessary.

4 If you will be on-line for long stretches of time and want Eudora to check your mail regularly, set the interval.

5 Set the width and depth of your message area and choose fonts for the screen and printer output.

6 If you want to change the directory in which to store incoming attached files, click on the Directory button.

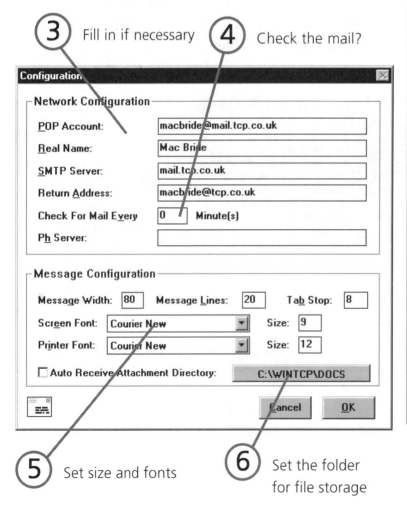

③ Fill in if necessary   ④ Check the mail?

⑤ Set size and fonts

⑥ Set the folder for file storage

106

Mail is stored in three folders – incoming and outgoing mail, plus a trash can. Deleting a message sends it first to the trash can, which you empty when you will.

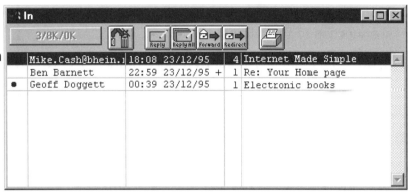

To send a graphic or other binary file, all you have to do is use the **Message – Attach Document** command and pick the file. The person you are sending it to should also have Eudora or a suitable converter.

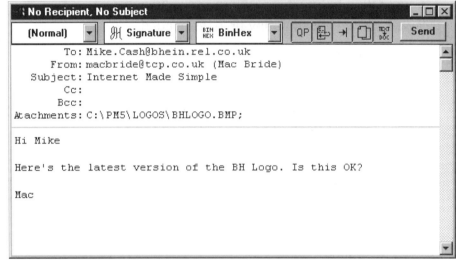

Take note

To use Eudora, you must have a POP3 (Post-Office-Protocol) account. Note that your account name will be different from your e-mail name/address.

Summary

❑ For Winsock work, you need a **fully interactive connection** to the Internet.

❑ You can use either **Trumpet Winsock** or the 95's own **Dial-up Networking** Winsock to handle your end of the network connection.

❑ The **Archie file locator** provides an easy way to find files, wherever they may be on the Internet.

❑ **WS_FTP** is simple to use, yet quick and efficient.

❑ The Windows-based **gopher** software requires little configuration before it is ready to use. Additional viewers can be added at any time, as needed.

❑ **Eudora** is an on- or off-line mail package, with a neat facility for attaching binary files to messages.

❑ All of the tools have a huge range of features and facilities that will keep the most advanced users happy, but can also be used easily by a novice.

8 The World Wide Web

Netscape

At the time of writing, Netscape is the newest and probably the best Web browser. It is quick and efficient, and though it has all the advanced features an experienced user could want, it is simple to handle. As well as managing the hypertext links between pages, Netscape can:

- display graphics in JPEG, GIF and other formats, whether from Web pages or stored on disk – and filed graphics can be viewed when you are off-line.

- access the Internet newsgroups, allowing immediate downloading of the current crop of articles in any group. This is a convenient way to get the flavour of a group when you are deciding whether or not to become a subscriber.

- link to ftp sites to download files. If you know the file's name and location, it is quicker and simpler to use a dedicated ftp program like WS-FTP, but Netscape is good for browsing directories and downloading.

- link into the Gopher system. As with ftp, dedicated gopher software will do the job better, but it is handy to have the facilities within one package.

Tip

Don't panic if your Web connection fails and you get a TCP Error message. It happens regularly and is not the fault of the browser. When you have links running through computers, networks and private and public telephone lines over half the world, it's a miracle they don't fail more often. Make a note of your current location, if you want to get back to it, and log off and start again.

Take note

Most of the screenshots in the next few pages were taken in Netscape 2.0, in its beta test version. You will probably be supplied with version 0.9 or 1.0. If you want a newer version, go to Netscape at:

www.netscape.com

Netscape opens at its **Home** page. The default will probably be your service provider's, but you can set your own start point.

Back/forward through loaded pages

Reload current page

Load images

Go to Home page

Open location

Stop loading incoming page

Print page

Current location

Find

Shortcut buttons

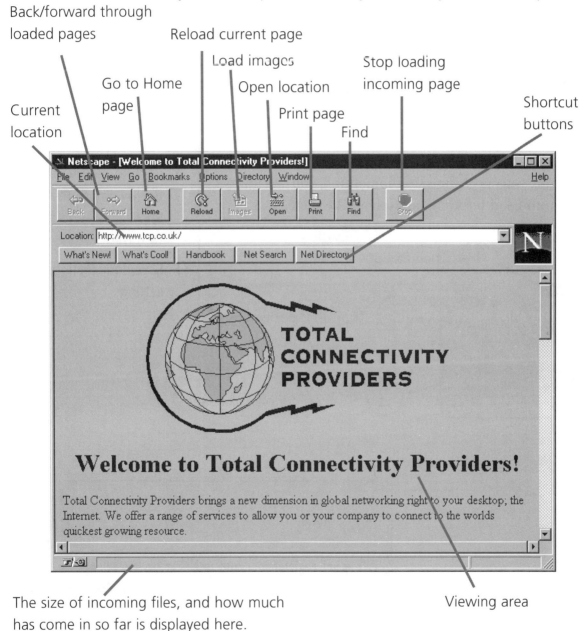

The size of incoming files, and how much has come in so far is displayed here.

Viewing area

Netscape options

You can run on the default settings at first, though there may be a few aspects you might like to configure.

The Toolbar, Location slot and Directory (and other) buttons can all be turned off, if you want a larger viewing area. The remaining menu commands will still give you full control.

Auto Loading of images can be a nuisance. Many images are purely decorative, but the size of the files greatly increases the time it takes to complete a connection. If you think you may be missing something, you can always turn Auto Load back on and Reload the page.

1 Open the **Options** menu

2 Turn off **Auto Load Images** for faster connections. You will then get wherever an image would appear.

3 Click to remove the tick by any of the **Show..** items you want to turn off.

4 **Save** your Options settings

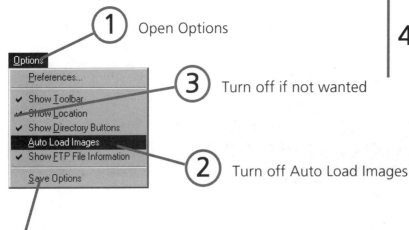

① Open Options

③ Turn off if not wanted

② Turn off Auto Load Images

④ Save your settings

Take note

When you register your copy of Netscape, you will get the Help file, otherwise you can only get them on-line. Once you have got them, save the pages, so that you have them at hand when you are off-line

Basic steps

1 Open the **Options** menu

2 Select **Preferences**

3 Open the **Helper Applications** panel

4 Work through the list and stop at any file type for which you have a viewer, but which is not already handled by Netscape.

5 Type the path and filename of the viewer program, or select it through **Browse**.

❑ Check the **Directory** panel, but leave the other settings at their defaults.

Tip

You can opt to save files for later viewing, or launch the application to view while on-line.

Adding viewers

Netscape's built-in viewers can display much of the incoming data, but there is a wide range file types out there on the Web. The more you can handle, the more you can see – and hear.

Check through the file type list in the Helper Applications panel, to see if there are any that you know you can handle with software already on your system. You may also spot some that you would like to be able to view. If there are, you can track down suitable viewers in the Internet's databanks and add them later.

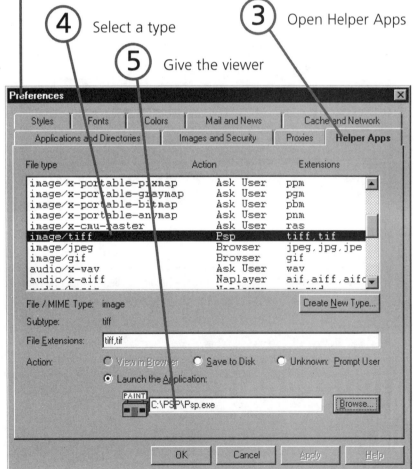

④ Select a type

③ Open Helper Apps

⑤ Give the viewer

Net Directories

One of the biggest problems on the World Wide Web is finding your way round its thousands of pages. Fortunately, several organisations have produced directories that provide mapped routes into the Web. The Net Directory button takes you to the *Directory of Directories*, which offer different starting points into the Web.

Basic steps

1 Get on-line and run Netscape

2 Click **Net Directory** and wait for the page to load.

3 Scroll through and select a directory by clicking on its name.

② Click to load

③ Select a directory

This is an advert – advertising is increasingly used as a means of funding Web sites.

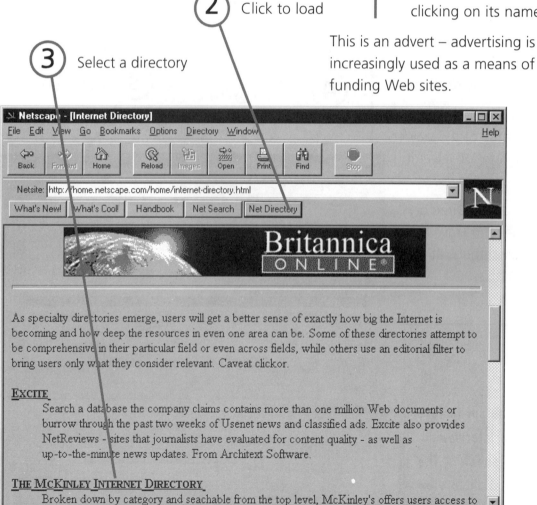

Yahoo

If an entry has a number after it, it shows how many pages are linked on from there; the @ sign shows a cross-reference; 'new' means new pages added in the last few days – and you'll find this by almost all entries.

Yahoo was started at Stanford University in the US, but is now run as a commercial proposition, funded by advertising and sponsorship. It has links to countless thousands (or millions) of pages, with more added every day. It has a comprehensive subject catalog, plus:

● **What's New?** to keep you abreast of the latest;

● **What's Cool?** including the not-to-be-missed *Interesting Devices connected to the Web*;

● **What's Popular?** and don't be surprised if you can't get through to these pages through overcrowding;

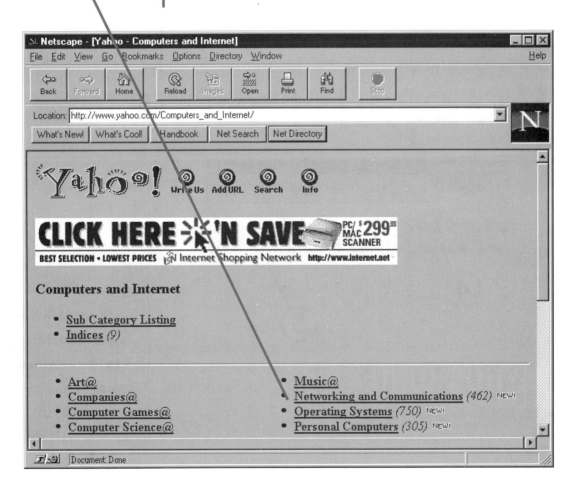

WWW URL's

Basic steps

Don't you just love the TLA's? (Three Letter Acronyms) The World Wide Web Uniform Resource Locators give the locations of pages. As the Web is so vast, being able to jump to a specific page is a great boon – and it is easy with Netscape. Let's see what on the BBC. Its URL is:

> http://www.bbcnc.org.uk

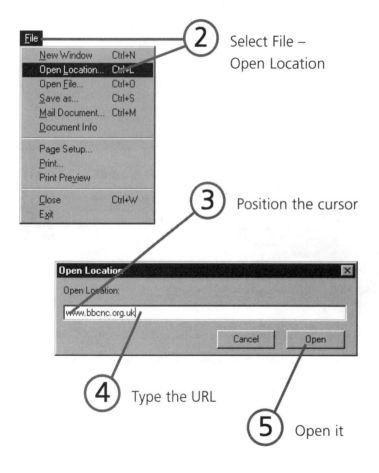

(2) Select File – Open Location

(3) Position the cursor

(4) Type the URL

(5) Open it

1 Make sure you have the URL to hand – they are not things that you can easily remember accurately!

2 Open the **File** menu and select **Open Location**

3 Click into the slot to place the text cursor there – it doesn't go there automatically.

4 Type in the URL, but not the *http://* prefix

5 Click [Open] and sit back and wait.

Tip

If you decide that you do not want an incoming page – and it's a big file that's coming in slowly – click on the red STOP button to cancel the transfer.

The Location slot shows the URL

Click the button to cancel a transfer

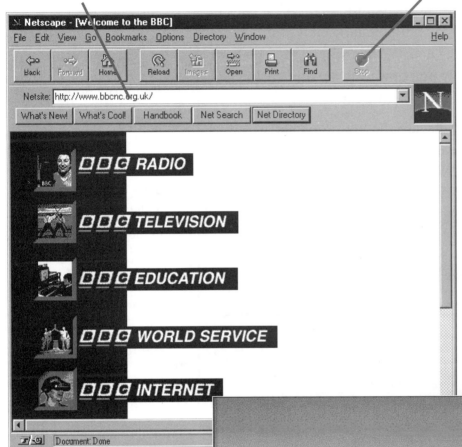

Auntie has really got into the Web. Her pages take good advantage of the possibilities of the newer Web browsers.

A shot from one of my favourite sites, the San Diego Bay Camera: http://live.net/sandiego

Late on a cold winter's evening, it's good to see the sun on the water.

Bookmarks

When you do find a good site that you want to revisit often, rather than write down its URL, to retype it back in later, you can add it to your Bookmarks. It is stored there as a recognisable page name. When you want to go back to the site, you simply pull down the list and click on its name, leaving the URL to the system.

Newer versions of Netscape handle bookmarks rather differently from Netscape 0.9 – the one commonly supplied by service providers. Newer Netscapes save all bookmarks in a file called BOOKMARK.HTM, and display them like files in a folder. In 0.9, if you want to keep them from one session to the next, you must save them as a file.

❑ **Add the current page**

1 Open the **Bookmarks** menu and click **Add Bookmark**

❑ **Jump to a Bookmark**

1 Open the **Bookmarks** menu and click on the page name in the list

❑ **Save Bookmarks in Netscape 0.9**

1 Open the **Bookmarks** menu and select **View Bookmarks**

2 A narrow panel opens. Click ⟨ **Edit >>** ⟩ to get the full-width panel

3 Click ⟨ **Export Bookmarks** ⟩

4 At the dialog, give a filename (ending .htm)

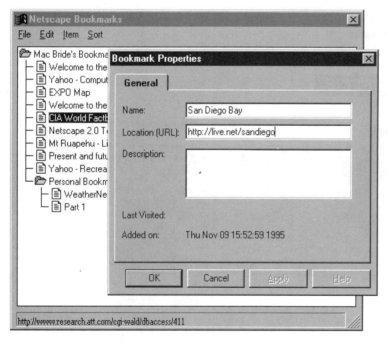

In Netscape 2.0, **Goto Bookmarks** opens this folder display. Options on the **Item** menu let you **Add** a new bookmark, or edit the **Properties** of an existing one – useful if its URL changes.

Take note

In all versions, you can have different sets of Bookmarks, saved as a separate files – useful if you are researching several distinct areas.

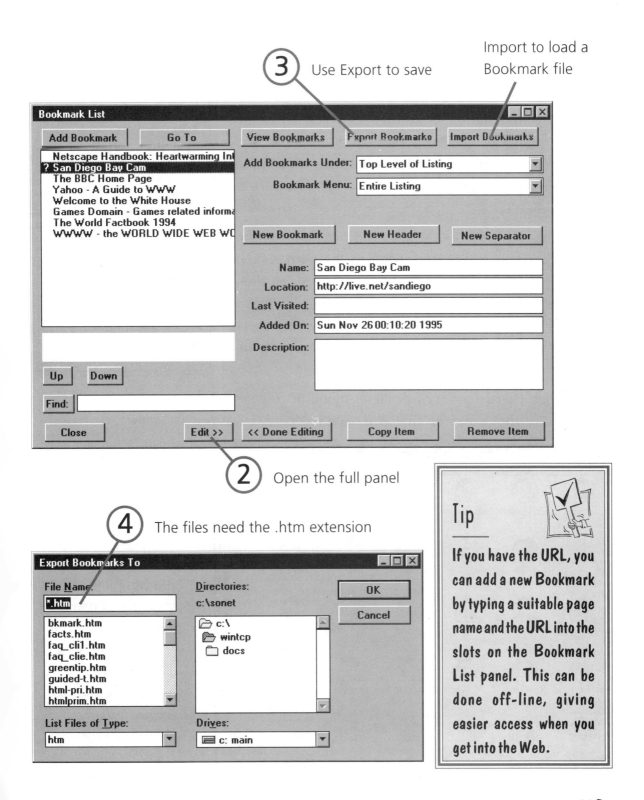

③ Use Export to save

Import to load a
Bookmark file

Bookmark List

| Add Bookmark | Go To | View Bookmarks | Export Bookmarks | Import Bookmarks |

Netscape Handbook: Heartwarming In
? San Diego Bay Cam
The BBC Home Page
Yahoo - A Guide to WWW
Welcome to the White House
Games Domain - Games related informa
The World Factbook 1994
WWW - the WORLD WIDE WEB WC

Add Bookmarks Under: Top Level of Listing

Bookmark Menu: Entire Listing

New Bookmark   New Header   New Separator

Name: San Diego Bay Cam
Location: http://live.net/sandiego
Last Visited:
Added On: Sun Nov 26 00:10:20 1995
Description:

Up   Down

Find:

| Close | Edit >> | << Done Editing | Copy Item | Remove Item |

② Open the full panel

④ The files need the .htm extension

Export Bookmarks To

File Name:
*.htm

bkmark.htm
facts.htm
faq_cli1.htm
faq_clie.htm
greentip.htm
guided-t.htm
html-pri.htm
htmlprim.htm

Directories:
c:\sonet

c:\
wintcp
docs

OK

Cancel

List Files of Type:
htm

Drives:
c: main

Tip

If you have the URL, you can add a new Bookmark by typing a suitable page name and the URL into the slots on the Bookmark List panel. This can be done off-line, giving easier access when you get into the Web.

Explorer

The Internet Explorer is Microsoft's Web browser for Windows 95. It has been designed – and is – easy to use.

- During installation it configures itself with the viewers it can find on your system. You can add more later, through the **View – Options – File Types** panel. The process is the same as adding viewers in Windows 95.

- During use it stores the text and images from the pages that you visit in a **cache** on the hard disk. If you want to go back to those pages, they can then be reloaded quickly from disk, rather than having to download again them. You can even revisit them after you have closed down the link, by opening the HTM file in the Cache folder.

- Though there are very few menu items or toolbar buttons, they cover all that you need to do.

Tip

Use View– Options – Advanced to set the number of pages to store in the History folder, and the amount of disk space to allocate to the Cache. Both can also be emptied from here if you are running short of space.

❏ Explorer also keeps a history (and the URLs) of places visited, so even if the page's file is no longer in the cache, you can jump to it by selecting its name off the History list. You can also jump to a page by selecting its shortcut in the History folder.

A list of sites visited in the session builds up on the File menu. You can also open the full history folder from here.

You can add your top sites to the Favourites menu for instant access

Change the size of the font used for the main body of text

To go to a new site, type the UTL into the slot and press [Enter]

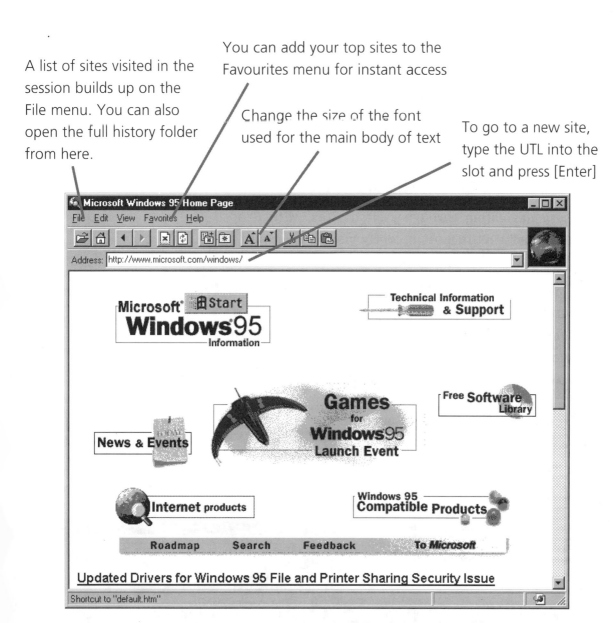

As Explorer comes from Microsoft, it seemed appropriate to go back to their home page for an illustration. They do create very attractive pages, but you need a fast modem to enjoy Microsoft's sites – all those pictures take some time to load.

Spry Mosaic

This is the Web browser supplied by CompuServe to its members. In many ways it is very similar to Netscape – all browsers share the same roots – but it has a few nice touches that make it very suitable for new and occasional users. These include:

- Ready made hotlists with over 100 page links – the computer and Internet related lists are very good.

- Easy navigating through visited sites, with drop down lists to the most recently visited ones, and a full history of your surfing.

- The Kiosk mode, in which the frame, menu bars and all the rest of the Mosaic interface are removed, leaving the whole screen for the page – excellent for viewing a large page.

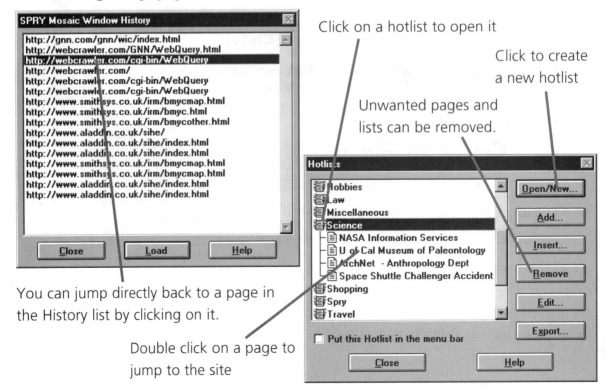

Click on a hotlist to open it

Click to create a new hotlist

Unwanted pages and lists can be removed.

You can jump directly back to a page in the History list by clicking on it.

Double click on a page to jump to the site

Open a file (off-line)

Open the Hotlist dialog box

Drop down lists of last
five pages visited

GNN has an extensive site
directory amongst other things

Kiosk mode removes the frame to
give a full screen view of the page –
[Esc] puts the controls back on.

Add current page
to hotlist

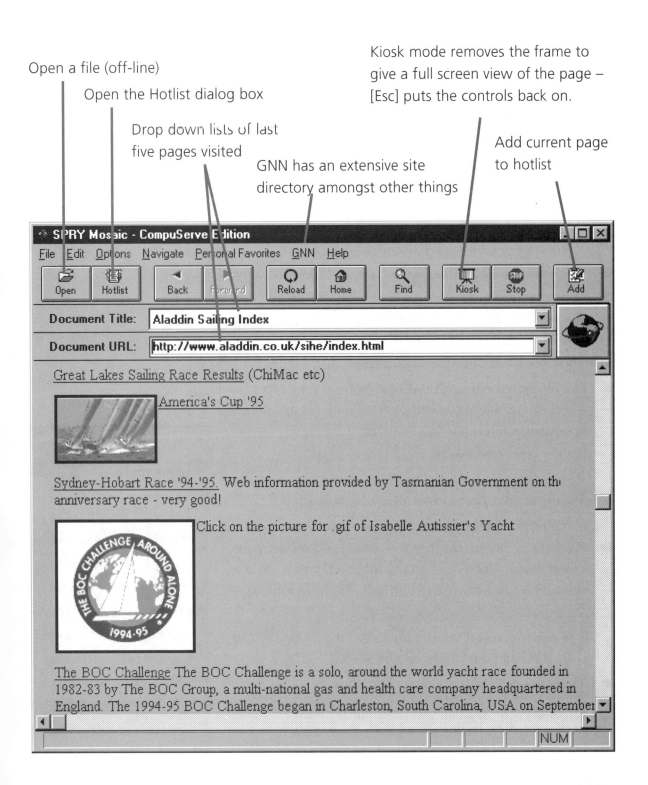

Hypertext

If your service provider offers you a free Web page, and you would like to take advantage of it, you will need to know how to create HTML (HyperText Markup Language) documents. It is not as hard as you may think. The documents are written as text files, with tags to indicate text styles and to link to other pages or files.

- Tags are written in <brackets>, and most are paired with one at the start and one at the end of the block. The tag is the same for both, with a leading / at the end. e.g.

    <h1>This is a first heading</h1>

- New paragraphs are marked by a <p> at the start only.

- Every document has two main blocks, the <head> and the <body>. The head block carries a <title>, which will be used in its Bookmark.

- The document must be enclosed in <html> tags.

- Images must be in a format that Netscape can handle – JPG or GIF are the commonest. To insert an image, give its file reference in the form:

    <img src="*filename*">

    If you include a path to the file, use the Unix / as the separator, not the normal DOS \ backslash. e.g.

    <img src = "/pics/mypic.jpg"

- To make a link to another document, either on your computer or elsewhere on the Internet, you anchor a reference to a phrase in your text. Anchors look like:

    <A href="*reference*">Key words</a>

    The reference can be to a file on your system, or the URL of a page anywhere on the Web.

- There is an HTML primer on the Web at:

    http://www.ncsa.uiuc.edu/General/Internet/WWW/ HTMLPrimer.html

Tags

<html> at start and end of document

<head> around title area

<title> Bookmark title

<body> at start and end of main text

<h1> First level head

<h2> Second level head

<h3> Third sub-head

<strong> Bold

<p> new paragraph

<hr> Line spacer

**
** Clear break

Take note

The pages you will see on the Internet all have the extension .HTML, which is four letters. The Unix systems that run the Internet can handle long filenames and extensions – DOS can't. Save files with the extension .HTM. Netscape recognises this.

To see how tags work, compare the text with the display.

```
<html>
<head>
<title>
Internet Made Simple
</title>
</head>
<body>
<BODY  BGCOLOR ="#FFFFFF" BACKGROUND = "madesimp.gif">
<h1>Internet Made Simple</h1>
<h3>Your Route Map to the World</h3>
<br>
<strong><p><img src="wincim.jpg" align = middle> <a href="compserv.htm">
CompuServe</a>
<p><img src="winnet.jpg" align = middle>WinNET Mail and News
<p><img src="tcp.jpg" align = middle><a href="http://www.tcp.co.uk"> TCP and
Trumpet Winsock </a>
<p><img src="winwww.jpg" align = middle>The World Wide Web
<br>
<p>
Plus: Communications, protocols, hardware and software, and where to find
service providers and tools for the Net.</strong>
</body>
</html>
```

This image is duplicated to fill the screen

Tip

To see how your HTML document looks, run Netscape and load it in with File – Open File.

Links to files in the same directory

Link to another Web page

<h1>
<h3>

<p>
<img src...
<a href...

Internet Made Simple

Your Route Map to the World

CompuServe

WinNET Mail and News

TCP and Trumpet Winsock

The World Wide Web

Plus: Communications, protocols, hardware and software, and where to find service providers and tools for the Net.

Summary

- The **Netscape Web browser** that it easy to use yet has a full range of advanced facilities.

- You must **run Winsock and login** before trying to get onto the Web.

- Netscape can also be used for accessing **News-groups, ftp sites** and **gopherspace**.

- You can control aspects of the display from the **Options** menu. It is often worth turning off **Auto Load Images**.

- You can add extra **Helper Applications** to increase the range of file types that you can view.

- The **Net Directory** button will link you to a DIrectory of Directories, which gives organised access to the Web. **Yahoo** is a good place to start your travels.

- If you know a site's **URL**, you can go directly to it.

- When you find an interesting page, you can create a **Bookmark** to get back to it easily in future.

- In Netscape 0.9, you must **save your Bookmarks** as a file before ending a session if you want them in the future. Newer Netscapes save them for you.

- Internet **Explorer**, from Microsoft and **Spry Mosaic**, from CompuServe, are good alternatives to Netscape

- Web pages are written in the **HyperText Markup Language**. This uses plain text with <tags>, allowing HTML documents to be written on any word-processor.

- If you want to see how a Web page is written, save it to disk, then load it into your word-processor.

9 Files by mail

Archie by mail

If you do not have an interactive connection to the Internet, you can run archie searches by mail. It may take up to a day for the results to get back to you, but at least you don't have to wait on-line while archie does its stuff.

- The mail should be addressed to:

  archie@*archie_server*

  where *archie_server* is any one of the servers listed on page 143. Example:

  archie@archie.doc.ic.ac.uk

- Anything in the **Subject** line is taken as part of the message, so it's simplest to leave this blank.

- Commands must start in the first column – leading tabs or spaces will kill a command line.

- To search for a file, use the command:

  find *filename*

  filename can be the whole name or a substring, as with interactive archie (page 100). Examples:

  find uuencode.com

  Specifies a particular encoding program.

  find ftp

  Guessing at the name of an ftp-handling program.

- If you give the whole filename, you can make it search for exact matches only by adding the command:

  search exact

  This doesn't just speed up the search, it also avoids having your returned mail clogged up with details of irrelevant files.

Tip

To get more detailed help on archie by mail, send a message containing the single word 'help' to an archie server.

128

Sample return mail from an archie search

There may be dozens of copies of the same file scattered over the Internet. This search turned up 14 files, including duplicates in different directories at the same site.

```
>> find uuencode.com
# Search type: sub.

Host nic.switch.ch    (130.59.10.40)
Last updated 04:13 25 Oct 1994

    Location: /mirror/msdos/starter
       FILE   -rw-rw-r--    997 bytes  11:07  5 Oct 1994  uuencode.com


Host micros.hensa.ac.uk    (148.88.8.84)
Last updated 03:30 29 Oct 1994

    Location: /mirrors/simtel/msdos/starter
       FILE   -r--r--r--    997 bytes  09:07  5 Oct 1994  uuencode.com


Host src.doc.ic.ac.uk    (146.169.43.1)
Last updated 08:30 31 Oct 1994

    Location: /computing/systems/ibmpc/simtel/starter
       FILE   -r--r--r--    964 bytes  09:07  5 Oct 1994  uuencode.com.Z
...
...
Host nic.switch.ch    (130.59.10.40)
Last updated 04:13 25 Oct 1994

    Location: /software/msdos/starter
       FILE   -rw-rw-r--    987 bytes  01:00 14 Mar 1991
uuencode.com
```

lines deleted

This is a file, not a sub-directory

Read/Write permissions, i.e. who can do what to the file. As long as it ends **r--**, you can get a copy of the file.

Size – useful to know before ftp-ing

Date – get the latest version

Filename

compressed by Unix – needs gnuzip or similar

ftp by mail

Having run archie by mail to track down the host, directory and name of a file, you can do ftp by mail to download it. This is not as convenient as interactive ftp, but it is a feasible way of getting files if you only have a mail connection. The commands are simple enough – the problems arise from the nature of the mail systems.

Mail is designed for text messages, so binary files have to be suitably encoded for mailing, then decoded on receipt (see page 132.) There is also a 100k limit to the size of files that can be handled by the mail systems, so large files have to be broken up into manageable chunks before sending – then reassembled afterwards.

ftp-by-mail requests should be addressed to the request handler at your service provider, or to:

    ftpmail@gatekeeper.dec.com

Example 1: A simple request for a directory listing:

```
connect ftp.ibmpcug.co.
cd /pub/WinNET
ascii
dir
```

Example 2: Getting MPEGWIN.ZIP, the MPEG video viewer:

```
connect gatekeeper.dec.com
cd  /pub/micro/msdos/win3/desktop
uuencode
binary
chunksize 100000
get mpegwin.zip
quit
```

This will come through in 8 bits, and must be patched back together before decoding. See page 133.

ftp commands

connect *hostname* – make the link to the remote system

cd or **chdir** *dirname* – change directory

uuencode – convert binary files to text

binary – switch to binary mode

chunksize *bytes* – size to chop large files into

ascii – switch to ascii text mode

dir – send a listing of the current directory

get *filename* – send the selected file

quit – close the connection

Tip

Stick to text files and smaller binary files at first - they give few problems.

```
REPLY-TO: ftpmail@ibmpcug.co.uk

total 1131
dr-xr-xr-x     2 root    daemon        224   Aug  3 11:30    COMPRESS
dr-xr-xr-x     2 root    daemon         32   May 20 17.23    FILES
dr-xr-xr-x     2 root    daemon         64   Aug 15 16:13    MAG
-r—r—r—       1 root    daemon       2934   Sep 13 14:26    README.NOW
dr-xr-xr-x     2 root    daemon        256   Sep  9 14:03    UTILS
dr-xr-xr-x     2 root    daemon         48   Jun 14 14:10    UUCP
-r—r—r—       1 root    daemon      12826   Sep 13 14:24    WinNET.txt
-r—r—r—       1 root    daemon      26400   Jun 20 11:07    internet.doc
-rw-r—r—      1 root    daemon      15561   Sep 12 11:55    internet.txt
-r—r—r—       1 root    daemon     202574   Oct  7 1993     pkz204g.exe
lrwxrwxrwx     1 root    daemon         10   May 27 13:42    readme -> README.NOW
-r—r—r—       1 root    daemon      10970   Aug 16 12:12    services
-r—r—r—       1 root    daemon      31824   Oct  6 1993     uudecode.exe
dr-xr-xr-x     2 root    daemon         80   Apr 13 12:28    v204
dr-xr-xr-x     2 root    daemon         48   Jun 15 13:04    win
lrwxrwxrwx     1 root    daemon         10   May 26 17:35    wn_news0.txt -> WinNET.txt
-r—r—r—       1 root    daemon     241211   Aug 11 15:23    wn_news1.zip
-r—r—r—       1 root    daemon     295408   Aug 11 15:23    wn_news2.zip
-r—r—r—       1 root    daemon     181866   Aug 11 15:23    wn_news3.zip
lrwxrwxrwx     1 root    daemon         12   Aug 12 15:37    wn_news4.zip -> wn_tools.zip
-r—r—r—       1 root    daemon     396214   Sep 13 12:00    wn_tools.zip
-r—r—r—       1 root    daemon     723693   Aug 11 15:23    wnmail22.zip
-r—r—r—       1 root    daemon       7662   Sep  3 18:42    wnmsgate.txt
-r—r—r—       1 root    daemon      70554   Sep  3 22:22    wnmsgate.zip
-r—r—r—       1 root    daemon      80553   Sep 13 12:00    wntools.zip
```

Mail returned from a **dir** request .

The characters in the leftmost column are:

d = directory – add its name to the directory path and **dir** again to see what's in it

l = link to another file – ignore these

- = text or binary file – you can **get** these; **ascii** if they end in *.txt*, otherwise **binary**

Take note

Requests to popular sites can take a while to be processed. I had to wait a week for one file!

Binaries by mail

E-mail is based on simple ASCII text, using only 7 data bits per character, the eighth bit being kept for parity checks. Binary files – pictures, programs and sounds – use all 8 bits of every byte. So how can you send binaries by mail? The answer lies in a very neat pair of programs, **uuencode** and **uudecode**. (*uu* stands for *Unix* to *Unix*, which is how mail travels on much of its journey.) They turn binary files to and from 7-bit ASCII text. If you join any newsgroups that circulate binary files, you will need uudecode, and encode if you intend to post files.

When you have downloaded the programs (from your service provider, or by ftp – see the previous page) move them into your DOS or Windows folder.

❏ **Encode and Out**

1 Exit to MSDOS and change to the folder containing the file to be encoded.

2 Encode with the line:
uuencode *filename*

❏ This produces a new file, with the same name but .UUE as the extension. e.g.
uuencode smile.bmp
produces
smile.uue

3 This is a text file. If you want to edit it to add a message, do so – just don't alter anything between the *begin* and *end*.

4 Your mail system may have a method of sending text files, or attaching them to a message. Use it.

5 Post the mail

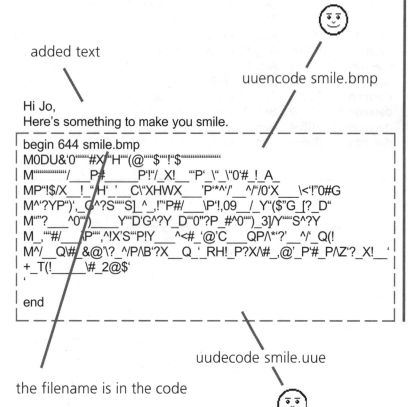

added text

Hi Jo,
Here's something to make you smile.

```
begin 644 smile.bmp
M0DU&'0''''#X''H''(@'''$''!'$'''''''''''''
M'''''''''/___P#_____P_!'/___/_X!___'P__!__A'_A_!_A'0#'#_!__A'_A_A'!_A'A'_A'_!_!A'_!_A'!__!'!'A_h'h'h'h'h'
MP'!$/X'_!___H'_'__C\'XHWX'__'P'*^^'/__^/'0'X'___<'!'0#G
M^''?YYP''';_G^?^'S'^''^'!''P'!',09__/__Y_'($$"G_[?_D'
M'''?'''_^0''''''''Y''D'G^'?Y_#'0''?_#'_^_''''''_3]/Y'''S^?Y
M_,''#"#'/P''','!X'S''!!!Y'''^<#_'@''C''''QP/\*^'?'____^'_'Q'('
M^^/_'Q'#_^'&@'\?_^/\P/\/'B'?X'_'Q'#_^^'RH!!!P?X___#'#',@''P_#'#'
+__T_(''''_\#'_2@@$'
'
end
```

uuencode smile.bmp

uudecode smile.uue

the filename is in the code

132

Basic steps

Binaries and WinNET

□ **In and Decode**

1 Take your mail and copy the section between *begin* and *end* into your editor, or copy in the whole message and chop off the surplus text.

2 Save the encoded part as a text file – the name is irelevant.

3 Exit to MSDOS and change to the folder with the encoded file

4 Decode with the line:

uudecode *filename*

□ This extracts the binary file, saving it with its original name.

WinNET mail has the encode/decode routines built into it, making the handling of binary files very simple.

When sending mail, there is an **Attach File** button in Quick Mail that leads to this dialog box. Just select the file to attach, and leave the rest to the system.

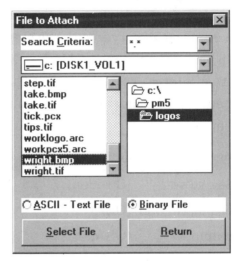

When receiving mail containing a binary, select the **Mail – Detach binary file** command, and give a filename. The system will cut out the *begin* to *end* part and decode it.

Take note

Mail messages and newsgroup articles are limited to 1000 lines. Large binary files may be split up over several mailings. Each part will be numbered and marked ---Cut here--- at the top and/or bottom. To decode these, you must cut out the encoded parts, stitch them back together in a text editor and save them as a single file. Run this through uudecode.

Gopher by mail

Perhaps the most intriguing thing about gophering by mail is that it is possible at all, but those of you who only have mail access to the Internet will be pleased to know that it can be done. However, patience is a virtue that you must possess for mail gophering. It can take a week to get to where you want to be.

The basic technique is simple. To start the process, send an e-mail to a gophermail server with the single message HELP. You will be sent back a menu. Mark an X by the side of any items that interest you and send it back. You will get another menu, or a document or whatever was pointed to by that item.

Use one of these gophermail sites:

gopher@dsv.su.se   (Sweden)

gophermail@calvin.edu (USA)

gopher@earn.net   (USA)

gomail@ncc.go.jp   (Japan)

Tip

Save the messages that you send, and if one produces a menu that you want to reuse, you can edit the message and send it again.

Basic steps

1 Address an e-mail to a gophermail site

2 Leave the Subject blank and write the word 'HELP' as the message

3 Send it

4 When the site writes back, check through the menu. If you see anything interesting, go into your editor to reply to it

5 Place an X to the right of the desired item, and mail the message back.

6 Save the mail in case you want to reuse the menu – it will save having to go back to the start.

7 Repeat 4 to 6 until you find what you want.

REPLY-TO: gophermail@calvin.edu

Mail this file back to gopher with an X before the menu items that you want.
If you don't mark any items, gopher will send all of them.

    1. About The World Menu.
    2. All the Gopher Servers in the World (long list)/
    3. Europe/
    4. Michigan/
    5. Middle East/
    6. North America/
    7. Pacific/
    8. Research/
    9. South America/
    10. The Home of Gopher, University of Minnesota/
    11. The InfoSlug System, University of California - Santa Cruz/
    12. Various Internet Systems and Databases/
    13. Weather and More/
X 14. Wonderful Finds/
    15. Worldwide Internet Phone & Address Directories/

/ at the end indicates a menu.

No / so these must be documents

REPLY-TO: gophermail@calvin.edu

  1. ACADEME THIS WEEK (Chronicle of Higher Education)/
  2. About the Wonderful Finds Menu.
  3. Coalition for Networked Information (cni)/
  4. Computer Services/
  5. Government Information On-Line from eryx.syr.edu/
  6. MTV gopher (unofficial)/
  7. MedSearch America gopher/
  8. The Electronic Newsstand(tm)/
  9. The Internet Hunt/
  10. The Internet Mall.
  11. US State Department Travel Advisories/
  12. United Nations/

Take note

There is a list of gopher mail servers on page 144.

Use the one that is closest to you, if possible.

Summary

❑ **Archie, ftp, gopher** and other facilities can be used through the e-mail system, though it will typically take a day between sending a request and getting a reply.

❑ **Archie requests** can be done conveniently by e-mail – and you don't have to wait on-line while it searches.

❑ **Binary files** have to be encoded before they can be sent by mail, so you will need uudecode to restore them when you get them.

❑ When **large files** are broken into chunks before mailing, and will have to be reassembled in a text editor before decoding.

❑ If your mail system allows you to **attach binary files** to your messages, sending binaries becomes quite simple.

❑ You can **navigate gopherspace** by mail, but it is very slow.

10 Sources

UK service providers

Aladdin   Tel: 01489 782221

e-mail: info@aladdin.co.uk

£25 registration/ software

£72.50 half-year, unlimited time.

BBCNetworking Club Tel: 0181 576 7799

£25 sign up, £12 month

Home & educational users only

Cityscape Tel: 01223 566950

e-mail: sales@cityscape.co.uk

£25 sign up, £15 month Unlimited time

Sign up fee includes registered *shareware*

CIX Tel: 0181 296 9666

£30 sign up, £15 month for 20 hours

Also runs an extensive e-mail/newsgroups conferencing service

CompuServe Tel: 0800 289378

£6.20 per month (5 hours) + £1.95p.h.

Free software and trial offer - see page 60

Delphi Tel: 0171 757 7080

e-mail: ukservice@delphi.com

£10 month (4 hours) or £20/month (30 hours) + £3 p.h.

DemonInternet Tel: 0181 371 1234

e-mail: sales@demon.net

£12.50 registration £10 p. month.   No time charges.

Take note

This list covers the larger service providers and some of the smaller ones with dial-in access throughout the UK.

The prices were correct at the end of 1995, but may well have changed – for the better. Increasing competition is pushing prices down.

The Direct Connection Tel: 0181 297 2200

e-mail: helpdesk@dircon.co.uk

£7.50 sign up £10 per month. No time charges

GreenNet Tel: 0171 713-1941

e-mail: support@gn.apc.org

£5 per month + £3.60 per hour peak £2.40 off-peak

IBMNet Tel: 0800 973000

£10 month (3hours) or £20 (30 hours) + £3 p.h.

Pipex (Public IP Exchange Limited) Tel: 01223 250120

e-mail: sales@pipex.net

£50 sign up £180 p.a.

PC User Group (WinNET Mail & News) Tel: 0181 863 1191

e-mail: request@win-uk.net (Subject: HELP)

£6.75 per month (Off-line e-mail/news)

+ £8.25 per month Internet access

Free trial offer - see page 82

RedNet Tel: 01494 513 333

e-mail: info@rednet.co.uk

£25 registration/software, £15 per month no time charges

Total Connectivity Providers Tel: 01703 393392

e-mail: tcp@tcp.co.uk

£7 sign up £10 per month unlimited time

Free trial offer - see page 96

Recommended ftps

General purpose tools

PKzip – standard compression/decompression utility:

ftp://kth.se/pub/tex/tools/pkzip/pkz204g.exe

WinZip – neat Windows version that Zips and Unzips (also handles files compressed by other programs):

ftp://sunsite.doc.ic.ac.uk/computing/systems/ibmpc/
windows3/util/winzip56.exe

uuencode – turns graphics and other binaries into text for sending through as mail or newsgroup articles:

ftp://micros.hensa.ac.uk/mirrors/simtel/msdos/starter/
uuencode.com

uudecode - turns uuencoded files back into binary form:

ftp://micros.hensa.ac.uk/mirrors/simtel/msdos/starter/
uudecode.com

Paint Shop Pro – excellent graphics conversionpackage, handling all the regularly used file formats. Can also be used for resizing, enhancing and manipulating images:

ftp://ftp.funet.fi/pub/msdos/windows/desktop/pspro20.zip

Winsock and Web tools

Trumpet Winsock – needed to handle a SLIP connection to the Internet, for Web browsing:

ftp://sunsite.doc.ic.ac.uk/computing/systems/ibmpc/simtel/
win3/winsock/twsk20b.zip

Netscape – Web browser:

ftp://ajk.tele.fi/PublicBinaries/msdos/winsock/ns16-100.exe

Take note

The Internet is constantly changing. These URL's were correct at the time of writing, but may no longer be so. The version numbers are the most likely things to change – look out for similar filenames when you reach the host directories.

WSArchie – Winsock-client file locator

ftp://dorm.rutgers.edu/pub/msdos/winsock/apps/
    wsarchie.zip

ws_ftp – Winsock ftp software

ftp://dorm.rutgers.edu/pub/msdos/winsock/apps/
    ws_ftp.zip

hgopher – Winsock gopher software

ftp://dorm.rutgers.edu/pub/msdos/winsock/apps/
    hgopher2.3.zip

Eudora – Winsock e-mail software

ftp://ftp.qualcomm.com/windows/eudora/1.4/
    eudor144.exe

Reference materials

"There's Gold in them thar Networks", by Jerry Martin

ftp://bells.cs.ucl.ac.uk/rfc/rfc1402.txt

"Hitchhiker's Guide to the Internet", by Ed Krol

ftp://bells.cs.ucl.ac.uk/rfc/rfc1118.txt

.. and many more (not always that up-to-date) at

ftp://mailbase.ac.uk/internet-guides

Take note

Most of these are shareware. Try them for free, but if you are going to use them in earnest, do register. It rarely costs very much and it does help to keep the flow of shareware going.

Major ftp sites

ftp.demon.co.uk (Demon Internet)

An excellent source of net tools and information – and while you're there you might look at what they have to offer as a service provider.

ftp.eff.org
The Electronic Frontier Foundation archives.

ftp.uwp.edu
Its **/pub/msdos/games** directory is a major store of games – and it is frequently so crowded you can't get in.

ftp.microsoft.com
Microsoft's ftp base. Search it for information and software they have released into the public domain.

micros.hensa.ac.uk
Lots of Windows stuff in **/mirrors/cica/win3/desktop**. This is a mirror (copy) of the main cica site in the States.

src.doc.ic.ac.uk (Sunsite UK)
– huge range of stuff, but a very busy site. Start from the **/pub** directory.

software.watson.ibm.com
IBM's public ftp site.

Tip

Pick your time carefully and you can download files faster. Avoid 7-11 in the evening, when you will be sharing your service provider's bandwidth with many other users. Avoid the working day at the ftp site, when you will be competing for the host computer's time with its local users.

Take note

This is a very limited selection of a huge number of sites, with the focus on those in or closest to the UK. A full list can be found at:

ftp://scitsc.wlv.ac.uk/pub/netinfo/ftpsites

Archie servers

United Kingdom

archie.doc.ic.ac.uk
archie.hensa.ac.uk

Europe

archie.switch.ch	Switzerland
archie.edvz.unl-linz.ac.at	Austria
archie.univie.ac.at	Austria
archie.funet.fi	Finland
archie.univ-rennes1.fr	France
archie.th-darmstadt.de	Germany
archie.rediris.es	Spain
archie.unipi.it	Italy
archie.luth.se	Sweden
archie.uninett.no	Norway
archie.ac.il	Israel

North America

archie.cs.mcgill.ca	Canada
archie.uqam.ca	Canada
archie.unl.edu	USA
archie.internic.net	USA
archie.rutgers.edu	USA
archie.ans.net	USA
archie.sura.net	USA

Far East

archie.wide.ad.jp	Japan
archie.hama.nm.kr	Korea
archie.sogang.ac.kr	Korea
archie.ncu.edu.tw	Taiwan
archie.au	Australia

Gopher servers

Some UK gopher servers

gopher.aston.ac.uk	(Aston University)
gopher.cranfield.ac.uk	(Cranfield Instute of Technology)
gopher.dmu.ac.uk	(De Montfort University)
gopher.ic.ac.uk	(Imperial College, London)
gopher.liv.ac.uk	(Liverpool University)
gopher.qmw.ac.uk	(Queen Mary & Westfield College)
gopher.bham.ac.uk	(Birmingham University)
gopher.brad.ac.uk	(Bradford University)
gopher.cam.ac.uk	(Cambridge University)
gopher.bham.ac.uk	(Birmingham University)
gopher.ed.ac.uk	(Edinburgh University)
gopher.newcastle.ac.uk	(Newcastle University)
gopher.nottingham.ac.uk	(Nottingham University)
gopher.wlv.ac.uk	(WolverhamptonUniversity)

Gopher mail servers

gopher@ftp.technion.ac.il	(Italy)
gopher@dsv.su.se	(Sweden)
gophermail@calvin.edu	(USA)
gopher@earn.net	(USA)
gopher@solaris.ims.ac	(USA)
gopher@join.ad.jp	(Japan)
gopher@nips.ac.jp	(Japan)
gomail@ncc.go.jp	(Japan)
gopher@nig.ac.jp	(Japan)

Tip

To find more Gopher servers, look for the Full list of Gophers around the world — it should be on the top level of your home gopher menu.

Index